Jenn Wilson

SAT*

Vocab Velocity

by Chris Kensler

Second Edition

D1558006

Simon & Schuster
New York • London • Sydney • Singapore • Toronto

* SAT is a registered trademark of the College Board, which is not affiliated with this book.

Kaplan Publishing
Published by Simon & Schuster
1230 Avenue of the Americas
New York, NY 10020

Copyright © 2003 by Kaplan, Inc.

All rights reserved. No part of this book may be reproduced or transmitted in any form or by any means, electronic or mechanical, including photocopying, recording, or by any information storage and retrieval system, without the written permission of the Publisher, except where permitted by law.

Kaplan® is a registered trademark of Kaplan, Inc.

Project Editor: Ruth Baygell
Contributing Editor: Seppy Basili
Cover Design: Cheung Tai
Interior Page Design and Production: Michael Wolff
Production Editor: Maude Spekes
Desktop Publishing Manager: Michael Shevlin
Executive Editor: Del Franz

Manufactured in the United States of America

October 2003
10 9 8 7 6 5 4 3 2 1

ISBN: 0-7432-4993-3

Table of Contents

About the Author

Chris Kensler grew up in Indiana and went to Indiana University, where he majored in English. He has written about politics, soap operas, and contemporary art. He has also authored over a dozen educational books, including the Word Whiz vocabulary-building book series. He has a pretty wife, two kids, four cats, and a dog named Joe.

Introduction

Do your eyes glaze over when you try to memorize lists of vocabulary words? *SAT Vocab Velocity* is full of words often seen on the SAT, along with far-out stuff you read about in magazines and see on television and in movies.

We've got celebrities—like movie star Brad Pitt, radio shock jock Howard Stern, and pop fave Mariah Carey, the songstress who never met an octave she didn't like.

We've got mythic figures—like eternal boxing champion Muhammad Ali, war-fighting man Norman Schwarzkopf, and home-run hack Babe Ruth.

And we've got history—looking back on folks like master thing-maker Ben Franklin and events like Woodstock 1—the first hippie love-in.

All we did to make this book practical was sneak a few hundred SAT words into the mix. Sorry. It had to be done.

But you know what? You'll learn the words without even knowing it . . . by using them to answer simple questions and to write short paragraphs about all sorts of stuff you might actually be interested in.

Feel free to skip around the book. You can't do it out of order because there is no order. Start with the stuff you're really interested in—music, movies, politics—and go from there. All the words used in the exercises can be found in the glossary at the back of the book. So breathe, have fun, and learn a bunch of SAT vocabulary words while you're at it.

How-To Manual

This book uses all sorts of exercises—fill-in-the-blank, multiple-choice, short-answer questions—to help you learn new words. Some are easy, some are not. You name it, it's in here.

What you need to remember is that for a lot of these exercises, the SAT words won't always fit their PRECISE, dictionary definition. You'll find yourself having to shoehorn a vocabulary word into a sentence or paragraph where you might not otherwise use that word. Remember, you aren't trying to win any writing contests here; you're just trying to get comfortable with these words and how they're used.

For the main exercises, write in or circle your answers right there on the page. For the extra exercises, you'll have to write out short answers, so do those in a separate notebook or on separate paper.

1. Gap-Toothed and Proud of It

In an age when you can change just about anything you'd like on your body, the perfect grin—white, beautiful, straight teeth—is being plastered on more and more mugs. Everyone from tobacco-chewing jocks to Hollywood actresses can have a picture-perfect pout.

Yet, standing for natural chopper pride is an impressive bunch of gap-toothed trail blazers who flaunt their imperfect ivories, challenging all comers. Talk-show host David Letterman, the Godfather of Soul James Brown, comedian Eddie Murphy, basketball player Scottie Pippen—even corporeal supermodel Stephanie Seymour—all boast an impressive space between front teeth numbers 1 and 2.

The following sentences about gap-toothed celebrities all have gaps in them. Fill in each gap with the appropriate SAT word.

1. Gap-toothed heavyweight champ Muhammad Ali was known for his witty _____, as well as his devastating left jab.
    a. aversions
    b. exasperation
    c. banter

2. Gap-toothed Flea, the bass player for the Red Hot Chili Peppers, often _____ the virtues of his bass playing idol, George Clinton.
    a. feigns
    b. extols
    c. hones

3. Gap-toothed, overweight, hair-challenged singer-songwriter Elton John looks _____ wearing his gaudy glasses, shiny tight suits, and earrings that often hang to his shoulders.
    a. invincible
    b. listless
    c. inane

Extra Exercise: Write a paragraph about one of the gap-toothed celebrities listed above. Include three words from the glossary.

2. Billie Jean King: One Giant Leap

Thirty years ago, sports fans didn't seem to care much about women's tennis; it was men's tennis that got all the attention. That is, until a female player named Billie Jean King came along. King single-handedly transformed the game of women's tennis, making it one of the few sports in which women earn as much as men. In fact, it may be the only sport in which that's the case.

King took the sport of tennis by storm. With an aggressive style of play and the strength to speak her mind in a male-dominated sport, she went on to win Wimbledon and the U.S. Open numerous times. In 1967, she was selected "Outstanding Female Athlete of the World." Ranked the number-one player seven times between 1966 and 1974, she had clearly elevated the status of women's professional tennis.

King's extraordinary success broke financial barriers as well. She was the first female athlete to win over $100,000 in prize money in a single year. Thereafter, she worked tirelessly to lobby for equal prize money and equal treatment of women in tennis, paving the way for multimillionaire female superstars like Steffi Graf, Martina Hingis, and Serena and Venus Williams.

So whenever you hear a loud *Goooxxt!!!* or *Rmmpppphh!!* coming out of the mouths of a couple of women engaged in a life-or-death rally, remember that without Billie Jean King, they'd be making half as much money and they wouldn't be on TV. In fact, without her, they might not be grunting at all.

Many of the enhanced opportunities for female athletes today can be traced to the lead of women's tennis and Billie Jean King. Write a short news article describing King's impact on society. Use the following three SAT words:

assuage—to make less severe, ease, relieve

paucity—scarcity, lack

exacerbate—to aggravate, intensify the bad qualities of

_____

_____

_____

Extra Exercise: Many of today's professional athletes know that they have become role models for the next generation. Identify an athlete that you know has gone out of his or her way to make a difference in the lives of young people. Use three words from the glossary to explain.

3. Jimmy Hoffa Never Made it Home to Grill His Meat

The day: July 30, 1975

The place: Bloomfield Hills, Michigan

The man: Jimmy Hoffa, former president of the Teamsters Union, recently paroled from prison

Jimmy Hoffa was the legendary founder and president of the Teamsters Union, a labor union for truckers and haulers. He was reputed to have mob ties and had been convicted of fraud. In 1975, after he had been out of prison for a few years, he was scheming to regain control of the Teamsters Union, then headed by his former protégé, Frank Fitzsimmons.

According to news reports, on July 30, Hoffa told his wife Josephine that he would be home at 4:00 P.M. to cook some steaks. He went to meet Anthony "Tony Jack" Giacalone, a reputed mob boss, and Anthony "Tony Pro" Provenzano, a Teamster official. Witnesses last saw him in the parking lot of the Machus Red Fox Restaurant in a nearby town. He was never seen again.

There are many theories about what happened to Hoffa that day, though his body was never found, nor was anyone held responsible for his disappearance. What do you think happened?

    a.   Giacalone and Provenzano **duped** Hoffa into meeting them, then eliminated him.

    b.   Hoffa was a **dolt**. He got lost on the way back from the meeting.

    c.   His wife Josephine is **culpable**. She ordered him rubbed out because he had called her "doll face" one time too many.

    d.   Frank Fitzsimmons was behind a **nefarious** plot to keep control of the Teamsters Union. Hoffa got in his way, so Fitzsimmons murdered him.

Answer: a. is believed to be the answer. Giacalone and Provenzano tricked (**duped**) Hoffa into meeting them and had him killed. Hoffa was surely not dimwitted (**dolt**) enough to be unable to find his way home. Neither was his wife likely responsible (**culpable**) for his death—they had been married for 39 years. Fitzsimmons, though, was no angel. He may have been behind an evil (**nefarious**) plot, even though he had once been Hoffa's best friend.

Extra Exercise: Life is full of unsolved mysteries. Write about an unsolved mystery that you are curious about, and provide some likely explanations using five words from the glossary.

4. Impeaching a President: What Happened

Former U.S. President William Jefferson Clinton was **impeached** by the U.S. House of Representatives in 1999. He had had what was **euphemistically** called an "inappropriate relationship" with a White House intern named Monica Lewinsky and had lied under oath about it. Many people thought Clinton had violated his presidential oath and should be expelled from office immediately. Others felt that Clinton should still be allowed to lead the country, though they didn't **condone** his behavior. What resulted was 13 months of exhaustive investigations into what the president had done to cover up his affair.

Although President Clinton was ultimately acquitted and not forced out of office, his reputation was forever **tarnished**. He was only the second U.S. president—after Andrew Johnson in 1868—to have been charged with high crimes and misdemeanors. Instead of being remembered as the first two-term Democratic president since John F. Kennedy, he will **infamously** be known as a president who blatantly obstructed justice.

1. Define **infamous**.

    _____

2. A **euphemism** is
    a. use of a small word or phrase in place of a large one.
    b. use of an inoffensive word or phrase in place of a more distasteful one.
    c. use of a funny word in place of a serious one.

3. **Condone** means
    a. disagree with.
    b. forgive; give tacit approval
    c. change.

4. Who else has a **tarnished** reputation?
    a. O. J. Simpson
    b. Reverend Billy Graham
    c. the Dalai Lama

5. Define **impeach**.

    _____

Extra Exercise: What would you consider an impeachable offense? Use three words from the glossary to explain.

5. Guess Who I Am?

1. I was born in Michigan, but I grew up in the sketchy neighborhood of Compton, California. That's where I started playing tennis. My dad ran a security firm and my sister and I practiced every day on the public courts. Sometimes we had to stop playing to run for cover when we heard gunshots. It was definitely a gritty neighborhood, a far cry from the **ostenatious** country-club worlds that a lot of aspiring tennis players are raised in. Lots of people thought my dad was crazy thinking I could become a world-class tennis player with such humble beginnings, but I guess they were wrong.

    a.   listless, lacking passion
    b.   showy, displaying wealth
    c.   confused, confounded

2. I turned pro at the tender age of 14. My dad had pulled my sister and me out of the junior tennis circuit years earlier, so nobody really knew if I was going to be able to compete with the world's best players. They thought turning pro at such a young age was an **impetuous** move on my part. They were probably right, but it turned out for the best. I couldn't play in the big World Tennis Association events until I was 15, and I struggled in the smaller tournaments for a while. But once I could play the WTA tour, boy was I ready. In my first 16 matches, I beat five Top 10 players—faster than any woman in history had ever beaten that many great players.

    a.   rash, impulsive, acting without thinking
    b.   well-reasoned, given to close scrutiny
    c.   careful with words, tight-lipped

3. The coolest part of my career has been playing wit hand against my sister. She's also a really great tennis player. We have both been ranked No. 1 in the world, we have both won a bunch of major championships, and we have both even beaten *each other* in major championships. Even if our careers are **truncated**, we have each already accomplished an awesome amount. And if we both end up having long tennis careers, who knows what we can do.

    a.   harmful, destructive, detrimental
    b.   exciting
    c.   shortened, abridged

Who Am I?

Extra Exercise: Using three words from the glossary, write a short paragraph about tennis umpires and linespeople and what the players do when the officials make bad calls.

6. Woodstock '69: The Original

"Something was tapped, a nerve, in this country. And everyone just came."

That from Arnold Skolnick, the artist who designed the dove-and-guitar symbol for the original Woodstock, a music festival that drew over 450,000 **slovenly pariahs** to a pasture in New York. The previous record for a rock concert? 40,000.

To this day, the Woodstock Music Festival is recognized as the pinnacle of the 1960s youth counterculture movement. It had originally been the brainchild of a handful of hippies, who, spurred by their love of rock and roll and money, decided to produce an outdoor rock music extravaganza. They had wanted to raise enough money to pay for a recording studio in Woodstock, a quiet town near New York City that had already attracted people like **liberal** songwriter Bob Dylan.

Whaddya know, it worked. Three days of free love, drugs, heavy rain, and little food. And awesome music. Performers included Joan Baez, Jefferson Airplane, and the Grateful Dead. And though Jimi Hendrix played the "Star Spangled Banner" on his guitar, it paled in comparison to the Monterey Pop Festival where, two years earlier, he had **kindled** his guitar, causing flames to rise high in the air.

1. If politically liberal songwriter Bob Dylan was also **liberal** with his lyrics, that means he
    a.   used a lot of words.
    b.   used very few words.
    c.   used curse words in his lyrics.

2. It is hard to **kindle**
    a.   dry wood.
    b.   dry paper.
    c.   wet shoes.

3. The author called the people who went to Woodstock **slovenly pariahs**. That means the author
    a.   thinks the people at Woodstock were neat and socially acceptable.
    b.   thinks the people at Woodstock were intellectual and progressive.
    c.   thinks the people at Woodstock were untidy outcasts.

Extra Exercise: You and your cosmic hippie friend, Moonbeam, have a hamster that has just given birth to quintuplets. Pick five words from the glossary that sound like groovy, hippie names.

7. Christina Applegate: Making It in Hollywood

Some actresses have all the luck. Christina Applegate is one of them. In front of the camera since the age of 3 months, when she played the pivotal role of "baby" on *Days of Our Lives*, Applegate has maintained nearly steady employment. Kmart commercials, and bit parts in movies and TV finally led to her big break: the big-haired, small-brained ditsy blonde role of Kelly Bundy on the misanthropic hit *Married With Children*. The show's success helped to solidify the Fox network's place with the Big Boys—NBC, ABC, and CBS.

At the end of the 1990s, in an effort to capture that Applegate magic, NBC bestowed her with her own sitcom, *Jesse*. Since that show ran its course, she has landed great roles in a bunch of movies, including *The Sweetest Thing*, *Wonderland*, and *Surviving Christmas*. With her mass appeal and talent, Applegate has indubitably shown herself to be a paradigm for success in a town where the *new* thing is often considered the *best* thing.

Pretend you had been a popular actor on the situation comedy "Is That Your Hat?" After 13 seasons, the show was canceled. You have just received an offer to portray a cannibal in the big-budget horror movie, "What's Eating You?" You have also just been offered the starring role in another sitcom, this time playing the sportive owner of a faltering tanning salon in Nome, Alaska. Which role would you choose? Include the following three SAT words in your answer:

quandary—dilemma, difficulty

predilection—preference, liking

tangible—able to be sensed, perceptible, measurable

_____

_____

_____

_____

Extra Exercise. Use three words from the glossary to describe how you would prepare for your chosen role.

8. Junior Johnson: Stock Car Hero

Richard Petty. Darrell Waltrip. Jeff Gordon. Their exploits on the auto racetrack have made them household names. They have enough Daytona 500 trophies between them to sink a small rowboat. And they have had enough endorsements to cover a herd of elephants with Pennzoil, McDonalds, and Kmart patches.

But they all owe a debt to Junior Johnson, the man author Tom Wolfe once called "The Last American Hero." The guy came out of Nowhere, North Carolina. He learned to drive fast running whisky from his family's illegal still over winding back roads in his supercharged Oldsmobile.

Then in 1963, all on his own, Johnson took a Chevrolet out against the NASCAR elite—including Glenn "Fireball" Roberts, Ned Jarrett, and Fred Lorenzen. All of those guys drove cars by Ford and Chrysler—companies that poured millions of dollars into their cars and their drivers. Chevrolet had pulled out of stock car racing and didn't spend a thin dime on Junior.

Junior didn't care. He kept driving his Chevy. In 1963, he won seven races on the NASCAR circuit—in a car he paid for himself and using parts he sometimes built himself. With his legend secure, he finally switched to Ford in 1964 when his car began to break down more often, but for those who had seen him in the early days, Junior would always be the man who took on the big boys—and won.

NASCAR focuses on one thing—speed. Write one sentence for each of the following four speed-related words. Set your watch and try to do it in under four minutes. Ready, set, go.

lethargy—indifferent inactivity

Sentence: _____

oscillate—to move back and forth

Sentence: _____

reticent—not speaking freely; reserved

Sentence: _____

alacrity—cheerful willingness, eagerness; speed

Sentence: _____

Extra Exercise: Before he achieved great success, Junior Johnson had been considered an underdog in his field. Everyone loves an underdog. What is your favorite underdog success story? Include three words from the glossary.

9. Carol Burnett: Ear-Tugging Comedienne

Legendary funny gal Carol Burnett has had quite a career on stage and screen. She is best known for her long-running sketch comedy show, *The Carol Burnett Show*—one of the most popular TV shows in the 1970s. She has also performed in several movies, television specials, and plays.

What the comedienne is probably best know for, however, is the way she tugs her ear at the end of every show. It began way back at the beginning of her television career, when she was a guest star on a children's show. As a secret "hello" to her grandmother who had raised her, Burnett tugged her ear. The greeting stuck, and when Burnett got famous, her ear tug did as well.

If you were a comedian and the host of a successful new TV show, what kind of secret greeting would you use to covertly communicate to your loved ones? Use the following four SAT words to describe who you would communicate to and how.

construe—to explain or interpret

unheralded—unannounced, unexpected, not publicized

voluble—speaking much and easily; talkative

allusion—indirect reference

_____

_____

_____

_____

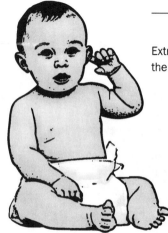

Extra Exercise: Who is your favorite funny gal? Describe her, using three words from the glossary.

10. Guess Who I Am?

1. I began my **illustrious** career as a bodybuilder. I pumped iron day after day until my body was a mass of sculpted muscle. I had a mane of tawny brown hair and wore Speedo swimsuits. I rubbed oil all over my body. I was a bronze god.

    a. easily influenced
    b. unchangeable, invariable
    c. famous, renowned

2. But being a bronze god was not enough for my massive ego. So I got into the movies, a career I had **aspired** to ever since I was a little kid in my hometown of Thal, Austria. My first movie part was playing the mythic hero Hercules. I was very good—fabulous, in fact—but they had to overdub my lines because at the time I had a thick German accent.

    a. hoped for; aimed at
    b. feared; loathed
    c. mocked; made fun of

3. Of course I soon conquered Hollywood. I was unbelievably buff and brilliant in action films like *The Terminator* and *True Lies* and I was a comic genius in funny movies like *Twins* and *Kindergarten Cop*. I married a Kennedy, too—a famous one but not as famous as I. I guess you could say I am a true **behemoth**, both because of my large body and because I conquer and dominate everything I put my mind to.

    a. legend
    b. movie star
    c. huge creature

Who Am I?

Extra Exercise: Write a paragraph about what you know about the actor described above, using three words from the glossary.

11. William Randolph Hearst: Big Man Media

He is responsible for tabloid journalism as we know it today. He has a castle named after him. And he is dead. He is William Randolph Hearst, who in the early 1900s, owned the most popular newspaper in America. His publishing and broadcast empire, The Hearst Corporation, still owns twelve daily newspapers and 15 magazines.

William Randolph Hearst was the man who turned "factual reporting" into "sensational reporting." He found that when he exaggerated and sensationalized the negative aspects of a story, he sold more papers. Soon, deception replaced exaggeration, and a new industry was born.

Hearst's motto was "Remember the Reader!" Make believe you are a newspaper mogul and your motto is "The Bigger the Word, the Better!" Write five headlines with the following five loooong SAT words. Here's one to get you started.

SAT Word: **countervail**—to counteract, to exert force against

Headline: Troops Countervail Attack, Force Opposition Back Across River
_____

SAT Word: **resplendent**—splendid, brilliant

Headline: _____
_____

SAT Word: **provincial**—rustic, unsophisticated, limited in scope

Headline: _____
_____

SAT Word: **legerdemain**—trickery

Headline: _____

_____

SAT Word: **malinger**—to evade responsibility by pretending to be ill

Headline: _____

_____

SAT Word: **ascertain**—to determine, discover, make certain of

Headline: _____

_____

Extra Exercise: Using five SAT words, write a mock newspaper article about one of the headlines you wrote. Don't worry about the facts being accurate, just try to squeeze five words into it. Remember your motto, "The Bigger the Word, the Better!"

12. Soccer Boogie

Soccer has swept the nation. The U.S. women won the World Cup, men's pro teams are drawing big crowds in a handful of cities, and kids everywhere are kicking the ball around just for an excuse to yell, "Goooooooal!" Hey, I bet you didn't know SAT words play a part in soccer.

Bear with me.

I am going to make a few statements about soccer using SAT words. Your job is to figure out what the word means. Pick a definition; for every one you get right, you score a goal! For every one you get wrong, the other team scores a goal! Whoopee!

The New York MetroStars swore they would **avenge** their loss to D.C. United when they met them again in the playoffs. They didn't. D.C. United beat them again.

1. **Avenge** means
    a. to retaliate, to take revenge.
    b. to make fun of, to mock.
    c. to lie about, to overstate.

Instead of passing the ball to his wide-open teammate, Brazilian star Bebeto **dithered** with the ball until a pack of fullbacks surrounded him and took it away.

2. **Dither** means
    a. to shoot on goal.
    b. to move or act confusedly or without clear purpose.
    c. to move with purpose.

After scoring the winning goal, Women's World Cup star Brandi Chastain **ingratiated** herself with the crowd by ripping off her shirt.

3. **Ingratiate** means
    a. to bring oneself purposefully into another's good graces.
    b. to chastise.
    c. to improve through hard work.

The two teams—Tom's team and Tim's team—were evenly matched. The team that won, then, would likely be the team that tried the hardest. Tom's team ended up losing because of the **lackadaisical** performance by its goalie, Ted.

4. **Lackadaisical** means
   a. inspired.
   b. adequate.
   c. idle, lazy; apathetic, indifferent.

France was able to win the World Cup in 1998 when it **quelled** a late-game surge by Brazil.

5. **Quell** means
   a. to crush or subdue.
   b. mimicked, copied.
   c. mocked, made fun of.

Extra Exercise: After you have scored yourself: If you won, pretend you are telling a reporter why you won, using the words **resolve** and **restrained**. If you lost, pretend you are telling a reporter why you lost using the words **dearth** and **prowess**.

13. Herbert Hoover Wasn't Such a Bad Guy Really

You've probably heard of President Herbert Hoover in the context of the Great Depression. He was the president who, in the 1930s, refused to give federal aid to out-of-work Americans who were desperate for food and shelter. Those Americans reciprocated by naming their shantytowns "Hoovervilles" after the president.

Before he mishandled the Great Depression, however, Hoover was known, ironically, as a great provider of humanitarian aid. During World War I, he was in charge of promoting agriculture and food conservation. After the war, he even directed the American Relief Administration.

Hoover was basically a hard-working, optimistic guy who thought that if everyone just worked a little harder, everything would turn out okay. Unfortunately for him—and for the country—the Great Depression needed more than people working "just a little harder." Hoover was never able to win public support, and he was labeled a callous and cruel president. He was badly defeated in 1932.

Imagine the country plummeted into a Depression today, with 25 percent unemployment, millions of people living in the street, and no end in sight. What kind of Big Idea would you propose to fix the situation? Use the following four words to explain.

benevolent—friendly and helpful

sagacity—wisdom

disparage—to belittle, speak disrespectfully about

myopic—nearsighted; narrow-minded

_____

_____

_____

_____

Extra Exercise: What if your plan didn't work? What would you try next? Use three words from the glossary to explain.

14. Guess Who I Am?

1. I was living in a rat-infested shed in Los Angeles when the second single I had ever recorded, a song called "Loser," was released on a small independent record label. Mixing elements of folk and hip-hop, "Loser" highlighted two very different styles of music I was quite **proficient** at playing. Somehow, the song got airplay on a local radio station, and before I knew what happened, everyone was singing it.

    a. extremely hungry
    b. dedicated, devout, extremely religious
    c. expert, skilled in a certain subject

2. The success of "Loser" set off a huge bidding war among the major record companies. Everybody wanted me. I'm a pretty **laconic** guy, so I wasn't really good at hyping myself up, but it didn't seem to matter. That song had everyone in a tizzy. They were calling me the next Bob Dylan and a spokesperson for my generation. Finally, I chose Geffen Records, and recorded my first full-length album, *Mellow Gold*.

    a. harshly shocking, sensational
    b. using few words
    c. vicious, evil

3. My second record was even better than my first. I played so many different kinds of music on *Odelay* that people just expected my music to keep being this eclectic mix of styles and sounds. But I do what I want, period. I am **intransigent** when it comes to my music. My next records, *Mutations*, *Midnite Vultures*, and *Sea Change*, could not have been more different from my first two albums, and from each other.

    a. uncompromising, refusing to be reconciled
    b. sparing or limited in appetite, restrictive
    c. well-spoken, expressing oneself clearly

Who Am I?

Extra Exercise: Write about your favorite pop singer using three words from the glossary.

15. Wisconsin: Got Milk?

Have you seen any of those smug magazine ads for milk? A celebrity is usually standing there smiling with a big swipe of milk across his or her upper lip. The tag line "Got milk?" is written somewhere on the page. Who's responsible for this ubiquitous ad campaign? Dairy farmers, that's who. Which state has the largest number of dairy farmers? The Dairy State of course—Wisconsin.

Nothing against Wisconsin—a bunch of my relatives actually live there, and they are truly wonderful people. And nothing against milk. My great grandfather was a milk man for 41 years. But that ad campaign really has to go.

Here are a few ideas for ad campaigns to replace "Got milk?" See if you can figure out what each word means.

1. I have a penchant for milk! A **penchant** is
   a. an inclination.
   b. something against.
   c. a strong distaste, loathing.

2. Milk cures your maladies! **Maladies** are
   a. sensitivities.
   b. troubles.
   c. illnesses.

3. Feeling depleted? Milk will rejuvenate you! **Depleted** means
   a. used up, exhausted.
   b. angry, bitter.
   c. happy, joyous.

4. **Rejuvenate** means
   a. to depress.
   b. to hurt, maim.
   c. to renew, to make young again.

Extra Exercise: What product is the state you live in known for? Make up five slogans for your state using five words from the glossary.

16. 1968: Riots in Chicago

For every year in which there is a presidential election, two conventions are held—one for the Democrats, one for the Republicans. In 1968, the Democratic convention was held in Chicago. During that time, about 10,000 anti-Vietnam War protesters gathered outside the convention hall to protest the Democratic nominee, Hubert Humphrey. Because Humphrey was not opposed to the war in Vietnam, there was a lot of animosity toward him among the protesters. The main anti-war candidate that year, Robert Kennedy, had been assassinated in California two months earlier. As protesters chanted anti-Humphrey slogans ("Dump the Hump!"), Chicago police officers descended on the crowd, and chaos ensued.

The riots were broadcast on national television. Chicago Mayor Richard J. Daley ordered the police to use tear gas to mollify the demonstrators. The Democratic convention was a fiasco. Humphrey ended up winning the nomination, but it was a hollow victory. He lost to Republican Richard Nixon in the presidential election.

Pretend you are a television reporter at the time of the riot and you are with the protesters when the police arrive. Use the following four words to write a television news report about the incident.

suppress—to end an activity

restrained—controlled, repressed, restricted

censorious—severly critical

ephemeral—momentary, transient, fleeting

_____

_____

_____

_____

Extra Exercise: Political protests have occurred throughout our history, including the Boston Tea Party, Martin Luther King's civil rights' demonstrations, and environmental protests by Greenpeace International. Protesters often use signs and slogans to get their point across. Use five words from the glossary to create your own protest slogan.

17. Tom Hanks: He Used to Wear a Dress

You may know actor Tom Hanks as the star of movies like *Catch Me If You Can* and *Cast Away*. What you may not know is that in the early 1980s, he was on a TV show called *Bosom Buddies*, where he played a guy who wore a dress so he could live in a women's-only apartment building (the rent was cheaper).

What if other movie stars had gotten their start wearing dresses on sitcoms? Following are some examples of what *might have been*. Using the provided title and SAT word, explain the show's premise. Let's start with an example.

Show title: **Counsel, I See Your Slip,** starring Brad Pitt as attorney Brenda Jackson

SAT word: **prosecutor**—person who initiates legal action or suit

Show summary: Brad Pitt stars as a prosecutor who dresses as a woman because

the city he works for needed to hire a woman.

Show title: **All Girls School,** starring Jim Carrey as science teacher Mrs. Rubberstopper

SAT Word: **noisome**—stinky, putrid

Show Summary: _____

_____

Show title: **Cowgirls Don't Cry,** starring Kevin Spacey as rodeo instructor Helen Horsewhip

Sat Word: **malcontent**—discontented person, one who holds a grudge

Show Summary: _____

_____

Show title: **Do What I Say,** starring Eddie Murphy as Grandma Iris Meaney

SAT Word: **imperious**—arrogantly self-assured, domineering, overbearing

Show Summary: _____

_____

Extra Exercise: Think up your own situation comedy using five words from the glossary. Think of what to name it, who will star in it, and what its premise is. Remember, with sitcoms, the wackier the better.

18. Jesse Ventura: From Wrassler to Governor

Jesse Ventura took the political world by storm when he came out of nowhere to win the governorship of Minnesota in 1998, **exploding** the theory that a former wrestler could not win a major election. Running against two political heavyweights from the Democratic and Republican Parties, Ventura ran on a third-party ticket—the Reform Party—started by founder billionaire Ross Perot only a few years earlier.

Few gave the former star of the World Wrestling Federation—who went by the name *The Body*—a chance to **fell** his opponents. But with a simple message of "no bull" and a slew of funny commercials, Ventura accomplished the **chimerical**, **confounding** the experts and knocking his political opponents out of the ring.

This wasn't the first time Ventura had reinvented himself. Before he was a professional wrestler, he was a soldier in Vietnam and a Navy SEAL—a member of an underwater demolition unit. And before he became governor, Ventura was mayor of Brooklyn Park, a small town in Minnesota, where he was also a volunteer football coach.

True to his party's name, Ventura worked as governor to reform the government in Minnesota. But one term was all that he could take. Running a state can wear out even the toughest ex-wrestler/soldier/SEAL/mayor/football coach.

1. In this article, **exploding** means
    a. debunking, disproving.
    b. blowing up.
    c. cherishing.

2. Define **fell**.

    _____

3. **Confounding** the experts means
    a. yelling at the experts.
    b. hanging out with the experts.
    c. baffling the experts.

4. What does **chimerical** mean?
    a. colorful
    b. imaginary, fanciful
    c. easily angered

Extra Exercise: If you were running for governor of your state, what slogan would you use? Use a word or two from the glossary. Here's an example:

"If elected governor, I promise to caulk every window in the state and to offer clemency to all convicted jaywalkers. Thank you! I love you all!"

19. The Hives: Perfect Punks

Just as the new millennium was getting its sea legs, punk rock punched its way back into the pop music mainstream. The Strokes, Sum 41, and Good Charlotte were all part of a new breed of old-school rock bands based on three chords, rainbow mohawks, and a killer sneer. But no one was better than The Hives. Five kids from Fagserta, Sweden, The Hives' had been kicking and screaming for years when the punk wave broke. Their record, *Veni Vidi Vicious*, hit like a "velvet glove with brass knuckles," according to one reviewer. Fast, raw, and sooo funny, The Hives were the right band in the right place at the right time.

And what a great name. Do they mean hives like bees, or hives like an itchy rash? If you were a fledgling punk rock group manager, what kind of band would you put together, and what would you name them?

SAT Word: **artisan**—craftsperson
Band name: Artisan Stench

Songs: This group of shower-averse craftspeople play ear-splitting homemade

amplifiers on songs like *Elmer's Glue Who?* and *Yarn Fight*.

SAT Word: **beguile**—to deceive, mislead; charm
Band Name:

Songs:

SAT Word: **cherubic**—sweet, innocent, resembling a cherub angel
Band Name:

Songs:

SAT Word: **dissonant**—harsh and unpleasant sounding
Band Name:

Songs:

Extra Exercise: Let's say The Hives performed at your school. Use five words from the glossary to describe this event.

20. Guess Who I Am?

1. I became famous hosting a radio talk show. I named my autobiography after my favorite subject—"Private Parts"—and even starred in the movie version of my own life story. I now enjoy **prosperity** beyond my wildest dreams. Big houses, fancy cars, lots of computer games—I can get anything I want. Isn't America great?

    a. respect, honor
    b. happiness, joy
    c. wealth, success

2. Every morning my on-air buddies and I talk about things that people aren't supposed to talk about. We've been called racist, sexist, sick, evil, stupid—you name it! We have the most audacious guests on the show— exhibitionists, celebrity wannabes, and other wacky people with ignominious ideas. Many listeners are shocked by these antics—and they can't even *see* what's going on! Maybe the only thing we HAVEN'T been called is **tactful**. I'll admit, we are about as tasteless as you get.

    a. considerate, avoiding offense to others
    b. tasteless, gauche
    c. patient, persistent

3. I'll try anything, and so far, I've been practically infallible; I just have what it takes to succeed. I'm an **intrepid** adventurer in the world of big-time media. I even considered a run for political office as governor of New York, but the public wasn't ready for my omnipotence, so I gave that up. At least it generated a lot of publicity.

    a. fearless
    b. first, primary
    c. fashionable, well-dressed

Who Am I?

Extra Exercise: Do you have a favorite radio show? Explain the show and why you like it using three words from the glossary.

21. Brad Pitt: His Love Life

Hollywood heartthrob Brad Pitt has had a few hits—*Ocean's Eleven*, *Legends of the Fall*, *Seven*—and a couple of clunkers—*Spy Game, The Mexican*—but one place where the bleach blonde smiler hasn't faltered is with celebrity girlfriends. Hooking up with actress Juliette Lewis early on, Pitt graduated to Oscar winner Gwyneth Paltrow before tying the knot with Jennifer Aniston of *Friends* TV fame.

Use the following words to describe some other famous celebrity couples. The first one is done for you.

Celebrity Couple: Brad Pitt/Jennifer Aniston

SAT Word: **propinquity**—nearness

Description: One thing probably keeping Pitt and Aniston together is their

propinquity—they both work in Hollywood, so they're very near each other.

Celebrity Couple: Elvis Presley/Priscilla Presley

SAT Word: **unappealing**—unattractive, unpleasant

Description: _____

_____

_____

Celebrity Couple: Lucille Ball/Desi Arnaz

SAT Word: **troupe**—group of actors

Description: _____

_____

_____

Celebrity Couple: Will Smith/Jada Pinkett Smith
SAT Word: **congenial**—similar in tastes and habits
Description: _____

_____

_____

Celebrity Couple: Clark Kent/Lois Lane
SAT Word: **vapid**—tasteless, dull
Description: _____

_____

_____

Celebrity Couple: Fred and Wilma Flinstone
SAT Word: **prudent**—wise, sensible
Description: _____

_____

_____

Extra Exercise: If you could date a celebrity, who would it be? Use three words from the glossary to explain why.

22. Jackie Chan: Star in Asia, Cult Hero in America

"Unlike American action heroes, Chan often takes his lumps, takes the easy way out, or even opts to run."

That from film critic Jami Bernard about Hong Kong action film star Jackie Chan, who has performed stunts like jumping off a bridge onto a moving boat and jumping off of a mountain onto a passing hot air balloon.

Serious stuff, and he does ALL of these stunts himself. No one can come close to this guy. He is the biggest film star in Asia ever, and he's had a bunch of hits in America as well, with *Rush Hour II* and *Shanghai Surprise*. The former was overdubbed in English, and in the latter he spoke his lines himself.

Sometimes SAT words can seem as though they're in another language. Here are six of the toughest words out there. Try using each one in a sentence that describes an impossible stunt Jackie might do. Underline the word and the definition in your sentence. We'll give you an example to get you started.

SAT Word: **propitiate**—to win over, appease

Stunt sentence: Jackie could not <u>propitiate</u> the muscle-bound freak, so instead of

appeasing him with his humor, he grabbed the chandelier, caught the freak

between his ankles, and flung him through a window.

SAT Word: **tyro**—beginner, novice

Stunt sentence: _____

_____

_____

SAT Word: **xenophobia**—fear or hatred of foreigners, strangers

Stunt sentence: _____

_____

_____

SAT Word: **megalomania**—mental state marked by delusions of wealth and power

Stunt sentence: _____

_____

_____

SAT Word: **inculpate**—to blame, charge with a crime

Stunt sentence: _____

_____

_____

SAT Word: **phlegmatic**—calm in temperment; sluggish

Stunt sentence: _____

_____

_____

Extra Exercise: Using three words from the glossary, write out script directions for an unusual film stunt.

23. Guess Who I Am?

1. I started out as a stand-up comic in California. My first big break came on the TV show *In Living Color*. It was similar to *Saturday Night Live*—a bunch of funny skits starring weird characters. People fell in love with my pyromaniac fireman character in particular and my physical comedy in general. See, I can bend like I'm made of Silly Putty. Unfortunately, **longevity** and television do not go hand in hand. The show lasted only a few seasons. I was out of work.

    a. long life
    b. good taste
    c. new talent

2. Luckily, I starred in a low-budget movie called *Ace Ventura: Pet Detective*. The movie cost almost nothing to make and earned over $70 million. All of a sudden, I was a big-time movie star! Unfortunately, my actress wife—who started her career on soap operas—left me for another guy! But that was okay. I have triumphed over **adversity** again and again in my life—hey, once I was itinerant. And now I'm making big bucks!

    a. bad publicity
    b. evil
    c. misfortune, unfavorable turn of events

3. Since *Ace Ventura* I've had all kinds of hit movies, with *The Mask, How the Grinch Stole Christmas,* and *Me, Myself, and Irene*. But it hasn't changed me. I'm still the same mercurial stand-up comic I've always been. I still use **spontaneity** in all of my comedy—when things get too planned out, they just aren't that funny.

    a. impulsive actions
    b. research and development
    c. elaborate props

Who Am I?

Extra Exercise: Using three words from the glossary, describe what you know about the actor described above.

24. Lost Generation Is Found

The phrase "the great American novel" got its start in the 1920s with a group of writers who lived, ironically, in Paris. Ernest Hemingway and F. Scott Fitzgerald led a rag-tag bunch of poets and journalists who were trying to put America on a literary map dominated by European writers and thinkers.

Dubbed "the lost generation" by their friend and benefactor Gertrude Stein, this group of writers went on to enjoy considerable fame and fortune. Together they wrote a slew of great American novels, including *The Great Gatsby* (Fitzgerald) and *For Whom the Bell Tolls* (Hemingway). Many died at a young age and Hemingway ended up shooting himself when he could no longer write well, but for a brief moment at least, they were the best writers in the world.

One thing Hemingway was known for was his use of small words and sentences. You could call him a kind of anti-SAT word writer. Following are some of the shortest words out there. Use the following four miniwords to write a short paragraph about your favorite writer or magazine.

ilk—type or kind

keen—having a sharp edge; intellectually sharp, perceptive

gall (v.)—to exasperate and irritate

ebb—to fade away, recede

_____

_____

_____

_____

Extra Exercise: Write the same paragraph using really *long* words instead. Fine tune as necessary.

25. Guess Who I Am?

1. As a **fledgling** politician, my first race was for a Congressional seat in my home state of Massachusetts. I won that contest, and my political career was on track.

    a. experienced
    b. beginner, novice
    c. bad, troubled

2. I ran for president against Richard "Tricky Dick" Nixon in 1960. We had the first televised debate between presidential candidates. I received lots of accolades—everyone loved me and thought I was charming, attractive, and coherent. But for Nixon, the debate was a **fiasco**. He got sweaty, he got defensive, he told stupid jokes.

    a. triumph, achievement
    b. good try, something to build on
    c. disaster, utter failure

3. As president, I had my share of good times and bad times. But then, I was the victim of a **heinous** act of violence. I was in a motorcade in Dallas when an assassin shot me from the window of a building. The nation mourned.

    a. typical, usual
    b. peculiar, odd
    c. shocking, terrible

Who Am I?

Extra Exercise: Write a paragraph describing what you know about the politician outlined above, using three words from the glossary.

26. Apollo 11: Eagle's Tricky Landing

Apollo 11's mission objective in July 1969 was simple: "to perform manned lunar landing and to return mission safely." In other words, to successfully land on the moon. There was one major hitch, however, as the Eagle landing craft descended to the moon's surface.

The computer guiding the astronauts' descent was **balking**. It was doing too many things at once and began to overload. Luckily, someone at mission control in Houston **grasped** what was happening, was able to keep track of the Eagle's flight path, and instructed the astronauts aboard—Neil Armstrong and Buzz Aldrin—to proceed with the landing.

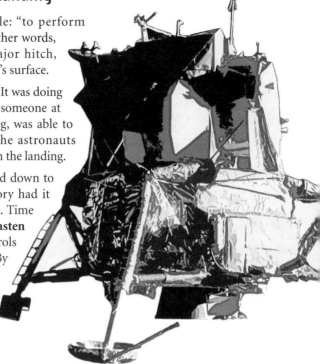

Despite more warning lights, Eagle precariously continued down to the moon. But there was one more problem. Its trajectory had it landing in a crater that was surrounded by huge boulders. Time was running out. Mission control told the astronauts to **hasten** their descent. Armstrong took over the manual flight controls and flew Eagle over the crater to a better landing spot. By the time it landed, Eagle was almost out of fuel.

When Armstrong's voice was heard over the speakers in Houston saying "The Eagle has landed!," mission control was **effusive** in its praise of the astronauts and then erupted in applause.

1. Define **hasten**.

    _____

2. **Effusive** means
    a. reluctant.
    b. jovial.
    c. expressing emotion without restraint.

3. The computer was **balking** means the computer was
    a. warming up.
    b. crashing.
    c. printing.

4. Define **grasped**.

    _____

Extra Exercise: Would you want to go up in the Space Shuttle if you had the chance? Using three words from the glossary, explain why or why not.

27. Friends: No One Told You Life Would Be This Way

Even if you don't watch *Friends* and feel sorry for people who do, you've probably heard of the show—six friends with eclectic tastes and temperaments who cohabit in New York City.

Following are short sentences about each Friend. It's not necessary to know who each one is in order to answer the questions, so give it a shot.

1. *Joey* is one funny dude. He has a pet duck and a pet chicken—in his apartment. He and his roommate had a foosball table in their kitchen. He is always joking around, playing games, and having a good time.

    Which of the following J-words best describes Joey?
    a. **juggernaut**—huge force destroying everything in its path
    b. **judicious**—sensible, showing good judgment
    c. **jocular**—jovial, playful, humorous

2. *Chandler* was Joey's sarcastic roommate until he got married. Afraid of commitment, he had trouble having a girlfriend until he fell for Monica. The only child of divorced parents, Chandler is usually suspicious of people until he knows them well.

    Which of the following Ch-words best describes Chandler?
    a. **chary**—watchful, cautious
    b. **choleric**—easily angered, short-tempered
    c. **choice**—specially selected, preferred

3. *Ross* studies dinosaurs for a living. An admitted geek when he was a kid, he scored big when he started dating *Rachel*. Then he blew it. During a rough patch in their relationship, the couple decided to take "a break." Ross thought that meant he could date a woman who worked at Kinkos. Rachel found out and dumped him.

    Which of the following R-words best describes Ross?
    a. **rustic**—rural
    b. **raucous**—harsh sounding; boisterous
    c. **rash**—careless, hasty, reckless

4. Which of the following R-words best describes how Rachel felt about Ross after she caught him cheating?

    a. **revelry**—boisterous festivity
    b. **revulsion**—strong feeling of dislike or repugnance
    c. **receptive**—open to others' ideas; casual

5. *Monica* is ultra neat. She can't stand to see a dirty dish in the sink or a dirty sock on the floor.

    Which of the following situations would likely send Monica over the edge?

    a. a **malodorous** bathroom full of germs and microbes
    b. a **magnanimous** roommate who pays more than half the rent
    c. a **morose** mother who calls every night complaining about her life

6. *Phoebe* is the space cadet of the group. Her mom committed suicide and she was left homeless, but none of that bothers her. She keeps her dead grandmother's ashes in a box under the seat of her dead grandmother's cab and sings songs titled "Smelly Cat and Crazy Underwear."

    Which of the following P-words best describes Phoebe?

    a. **parochial**—limited in scope or outlook, provincial
    b. **pallid**—lacking color or liveliness
    c. **plucky**—courageous, spunky

Extra Exercise: Write a short article about your favorite TV star using three of the words defined above.

28. The Guggenheim Museum

Designed by architect extraordinaire Frank Lloyd Wright in the 1950s, the Guggenheim Museum in New York City is one of the most famous buildings on the planet. A kind of massive concrete corkscrew, the museum displays its art on a long, winding path that circles up and up. The art that is housed in the museum is also abstract, as you can tell from the Guggenheim's original name: the Museum of Non-Objective Painting (huh?). This name reflected Wright's desire to create an environment that would make visitors feel as though they had entered another world—a type of contemplative haven. In fact, the museum had the most sophisticated sound system available at the time, making it the first museum to combine architecture, art, and music.

Pretend you are designing a freaky museum and putting freaky art in it. First, sketch the building. Then, sketch a piece of art you might put in it.

Freaky Museum

Freaky Art

Let's say you had attended the museum's opening. You spoke with some art critics over a plate of cheese and a glass of punch. Answer with the most appropriate response.

1. *Critic 1:*   I **revile** the design of your museum! What were you thinking?

    Answer a.   Thank you. I'm glad you like it!
    Answer b.   How dare you insult me at my opening. Get out!
    Answer c.   Mostly I was thinking about goats.

2. *Critic 2:*   The art is wonderfully new and aggressive, and **spurns** everything that came before. Bravo!

    Answer a.   Yes, the artist pays homage to all other forms of painting.
    Answer b.   You are right. It is unlike any other art out there today.
    Answer c.   Didn't I already tell you to leave? Get out!

3. *Critic 3:*   I can **infer** from the inchoate art displayed here that these artists have a paucity of talent.

    Answer a.   Oh really? Hmm. Well, you may have a point there old chum.
    Answer b.   I know. Their talent is laudable.
    Answer c.   I love you Critic 3. Marry me now!

4. *Critic 4:*   Please **expound** on your theories of life, art, and commerce.

    Answer a.   Fine. I will keep my theories to myself, as you request.
    Answer b.   Fine. Just let me find my sketchpad and I'll start drawing.
    Answer c.   Fine. Life is a bowl of bing cherries, and art is the stem, while commerce is the pit!

Extra Exercise: Expound on your theories of life using three words from the glossary. Make your theories as overblown as you want. Theories are better that way.

29. The Great Communicator

Former U.S. President Ronald Reagan was known as the *Great Communicator*. A former Hollywood movie star, Reagan was very comfortable in front of cameras; he used that to his advantage as president, delivering great speeches and telling stories whenever he got the chance.

One of Reagan's most famous speeches was in front of the Berlin Wall in 1987. Back then, Germany was divided in half—one half was communist, the other half was capitalist. Reagan took a trip to the capitalist side—West Germany—and made a speech directed at Mikhail Gorbachev, the leader of the Soviet Union.

> "…if you seek peace, if you seek prosperity for the Soviet Union and Eastern Europe, if you seek liberalization, come here to this gate. Mr. Gorbachev, open this gate! Mr. Gorbachev, tear down this wall!"

Two years later, it happened.

Pretend you are a speechwriter for the current president. Use the following three SAT words to write a short but strong speech about something you think the president should take a stand on. We'll get you started.

wary—careful, cautious

sanguine—cheerfully optimistic; ruddy

querulous—inclined to complain, irritable

My fellow Americans, _____

_____

_____

_____

Extra Exercise: If you were president, what national problem would you make your first priority? Using four words from the glossary, describe the problem and what you would do to fix it.

30. Buckaroo Bonzai: A Cowboy's Gotta Live

The American cowboy, mythologized in movies and television as a noble, self-sufficient he-man type, was actually the lowest of the low when it came to jobs back in the late 1800s. For three or four months work moving thousands of cattle across hundreds of miles of scary-as-all-get-out terrain, a cowboy earned about $100.

But what he did with that $100 made it all worthwhile. Usually, it involved a skanky room at an inn, a bath, a shave, and a maelstrom of late-night partying. In many cowboy towns, saloons outnumbered other buildings.

Pretend you own an inn that caters to cowboys with $100 to blow. You stand outside beckoning feckless buckaroos to spend their hard-earned dollars at your fine establishment. Use the following SAT words in a sentence to entice the inebriated cowpoke. We'll get you started with an example.

SAT Word: **habitat**—dwelling place

Invitation: Come on in cowboy! The habitat I have here was built just for you. Hot

and cold running water and whiskey!

SAT Word: **kudos**—fame, glory, honor

Invitation: _____

_____

_____

SAT Word: **mirth**—frivolity, gaiety, laughter

Invitation: _____

_____

_____

SAT Word: **palatial**—like a palace, magnificent

Invitation: _____

_____

_____

Extra Exercise: Imagine you are a cowboy/cowgirl who has just come off a three-month cattle drive. How would spend your $100? Include three words from the glossary.

31. Watergate: More Than Just a Presidential Scandal

You probably know Watergate as the odious scandal that brought down a president—Richard Nixon to be exact. You probably know that Watergate involved the president's lying, cheating, and paying people off. That's why he had to quit the presidency.

But do you know what Watergate actually is? It's a hotel in Washington, DC. The scandal was called "Watergate" because that's the hotel Nixon's henchmen broke into during the 1972 presidential campaign. They broke into the opposition Democratic National Committee headquarters there in an attempt to gather intelligence and plant a bugging device that would tap into phone conversations. The hotel is still there. Lots of big-time politicians live there.

Pretend you are a real estate broker and you have to rent out rooms in the Watergate Hotel. Use the following statistics to create an advertisement for the hotel, along with the following three words.

* 232-room luxury hotel
* 12 presidential suites
* 2 restaurants in building
* Walking distance to all national monuments
* Opened in 1967

hedonist—person who pursues pleasure as a goal

pretentious—pretending to be important, intelligent or cultured

reclusive—shut off from the world

_____

_____

_____

_____

Extra Exercise: If you were a president who had broken the law, would you cover up your crime? Or would you confess and let the American people decide your fate? Use three words from the glossary to answer the question.

32. Guess Who I Am?

1. I got my start in the movies in George Lucas's first movie. No, it wasn't *Star Wars*—it was *American Graffiti*, a story about teenage life in the 1950s. I played a hood, a greaser, a punk. The movie was a big hit, and people started to recognize me, but it was nothing compared to the **adulation** I would get after the next movie I starred in.

   a. high praise
   b. hot dates
   c. high salary

2. *Star Wars* was my next movie. I played Han Solo, a **winsome,** wisecracking spaceship pilot. It was a dream role. Not only was I charming and salubrious, I played opposite a walking carpet named Chewbacca. That made me look even better.

   a. weary, tired
   b. careless
   c. charming, happily engaging

3. Then came my REALLY big break—acting for Steven Spielberg in *Raiders of the Lost Ark*. That movie and *Star Wars* are both in the top-ten, all-time **grossing** movies. And I starred in BOTH of them. Those two movies made so much money, people were begging me to be in their movies after that. Am I lucky or what?

   a. disgusting
   b. totaling
   c. best reviewed

Who Am I?

Extra Exercise: Using three words from the glossary, decribe what you know about the actor described above.

33. Hot Dog Jungle

Mmm mmmm! There's nothing like a big, juicy, hot dog on a hot summer day. Seasoned cow, chicken, and pig bodies—and tasty body parts too, like feet, intestines, even knees—all compressed into one long mouthful! Yummy stuff.

A hundred years back, you couldn't trust your hot dog the way you can today. Decayed meat, tubercular meat, rat meat—it was all used. That is, until a novelist named Upton Sinclair wrote the best-selling book *The Jungle* in 1906 about the Chicago meat packing industry. Things shaped up after that, so now you know that your pig, chicken, and beef scraps are free and clear of disease and decay.

Does it ever freak you out to think about what you put in your body? Pretend you are an advertising executive and you have to come up with marketing slogans for the following products. Use the word that's provided in your slogan. We'll get you started with an example.

Food Product: Fried Horse Lips

SAT Word: **quadruped**—animal having four feet

Advertising Slogan: Running on empty? Eat a quadruped! Fried horse lips will help

get you to the finish line.

Food Product: White Dove Pops

SAT Word: **sybarite**—person devoted to pleasure and luxury

Advertising Slogan:

Food Product: Gecko Gum Drops

SAT Word: **nutritive**—relating to nutrition or health

Advertising Slogan:

Food Product: Chocolate Covered Toe Webbing
SAT Word: **wan**—sickly pale

Advertising Slogan: _____

_____

Food Product: Seasoned Bat Knees
SAT Word: **affront**—personal offense; insult

Advertising Slogan: _____

_____

Food Product: Stuffed Fish Tummies
SAT Word: **turgid**—swollen, bloated

Advertising Slogan: _____

_____

Food Product: Lizard Jerky
SAT Word: **iota**—very tiny amount

Advertising Slogan: _____

_____

Extra Exercise: Have you ever considered becoming a vegetarian? Using three words from the glossary, explain why you would or wouldn't consider it.

34. Andy Warhol: Soup Cans . . . and So Much More

Pop artist Andy Warhol is most famous for painting pictures of Campbell's Soup cans and movie star Marilyn Monroe. Oh yeah—and for wearing a blonde wig. Warhol spent the 1970s and 1980s mass-producing images of American consumer goods and flashy celebrity portraits in order to reflect the hollowness of American material culture. He also predicted that everyone would have "15 minutes of fame."

Did you know, however, that the artist also made movies, produced records, and drew advertisements for magazines?

If you were a multitalented artist, what would you create? Use the following words to describe your contributions to the following media. We'll start you out with an example.

TV Show: A sitcom in which a small baby has the brain of a nuclear scientist

SAT Words: **quadrilateral**—four-sided polygon

                  pellucid—transparent; translucent; easily understood

Show Title: **Nuclear Family**

Description: Baby Ned Needlenut is born with the ability to perform the complex equations necessary to build a nuclear bomb. His first word was "quadrilateral," which he said after his mother gave him a wheat thin for teething. For baby Ned, even the most difficult math problems are pellucid. Naturally, every country now wants him for its nuclear research program, but he still can't figure out how to use the potty.

Film: A movie about your best friend on the lam from some mobsters because he stole the money they were making selling tax-free cigarettes

SAT Words: **neonate**—newborn child

                  obsequy—funeral ceremony

Film Title: _____

Description: _____

_____

_____

Compact Disc: A collection of tunes by your favorite local band

SAT Words: **pastiche**—piece of literature or music imitating other works

                sobriquet—nickname

CD Title: _____

Description: _____

_____

_____

Painting: 10-foot high mural of your favorite breakfast cereal

SAT Words: **morsel**—small bit of food

                novitiate—state of being a beginner or novice

Painting Title: _____

Description: _____

_____

_____

Extra Exercise: Write a short fictional biography of yourself as a multitalented, wig-wearing artist who created all of the art above. Use three of the words listed above.

35. Reverend Jesse Jackson: A Life of Service

The civil rights leader and two-time presidential candidate Jesse Jackson was born Jesse Louis Burns on October 8, 1941. After his biological father initially refused to acknowledge him, he took his stepfather's name, Jackson. After attending university, Jackson became a civil rights leader in 1963. In 1965, Jackson headed to Selma, Alabama where he asked the Reverend Martin Luther King for a job in his Civil Rights organization. Jackson rose through the ranks and became national director of the organization in 1967. In 1968, he was **ordained**, and has continued to work in the name of God for the equal rights of all ever since.

An **articulate** and impressive orator, Jackson used his talent for public speaking to become a national leader in the quest for Civil Rights. Called "the conscience of the nation" and "the great unifier," Jackson has worked for **multifarious** causes, from freeing American hostages and servicemen overseas; to founding the National Rainbow Coalition; to hosting his own talk show. A **munificent** leader, he has given himself fully to his causes and the people who need him most.

1. Why is it important for an orator to be **articulate**?

   a. because one who speaks publicly should be good with words.
   b. because one who speaks publicly should be well groomed.
   c. because one who speaks publicly should be kind and generous.

2. **Multifarious** means

   a. righteous.
   b. beneficial.
   c. diverse.

3. Define **munificent**.

   _____

4. Who else is **ordained**?

   a. retired basketball star Michael Jordan
   b. the president
   c. Reverend Jerry Falwell

Extra Exercise: Jesse Jackson has devoted his life to improving the lives of African Americans. What cause would you devote your life to? Use three words from the glossary.

36. Mae West Was the Best

A film and theater star in the 1930s, Mae West was known for her racy language and enormous appeal. What is perhaps most impressive about her though is that she wrote all of her own lines—well, most of them anyway. One of the reasons she appeared in so few films—12 over a career that spanned more than 50 years—was that she insisted on complete creative control for all of her characters, which meant she rewrote all of her lines. Usually for the better. Among her classic lines are:

"It is better to be looked over than overlooked."

"Between two evils, I always pick the one I never tried before."

"I'm no model lady. A model's just an imitation of the real thing."

See if you can come up with some witty one-liners using the following SAT words. We'll get you started:

SAT word: **quiver**—to shake slightly, tremble

Our quip: Most people quiver when they get cold, but I'm not most people.
_____

SAT word: **conventional**—typical, customary

Your quip: _____

SAT word: **coquette**—woman who flirts

Your quip: _____

SAT word: **pious**—dedicated, devout, extremely religious

Your quip: _____

Extra Exercise: Who is your favorite comedian? Describe him or her using three words from the glossary. Try to include a few quips you think are particularly funny.

37. Lockdown USA: Prison Overcrowding

The 1990s saw the United States jail more people than ever before in its history. As incarceration rates grew, sentences also became longer, especially for nonviolent crimes. But while people were being locked up at record rates, new prison construction was not keeping pace. That meant serious overcrowding of prisons and jails. Prison hallways, chapels—even bathrooms—were used to house the overflow of inmates.

Imagine you are a U.S. Senator and you must present a speech to Congress about prison overcrowding. Using the SAT word provided, write a topic sentence to start each of the four following speeches.

Senate Speech: Inmates Deserve Everything They Get
SAT word: **incarcerate**—to put in jail, confine

_____

Senate Speech: No One Should Have to Live in a Bathroom
SAT word: **incense**—to infuriate, enrage

_____

Senate Speech: You Don't Want to Share a Toilet With 27 People?
Then Don't Break the Law!
SAT word: **finicky**—fussy, difficult to please

_____

Senate Speech: Nonviolent Criminals Shouldn't Go to Prison—Period
SAT word: **exculpate**—to clear of blame or fault, vindicate

_____

Extra Exercise: Using three words from the glossary, describe one thing that you believe would effectively deter criminals from a life of crime.

38. Guess Who I Am?

1. I started playing golf when I was incredibly young—two years old to be exact. My dad wanted me to the best golfer ever. When I was five, I went on *The Tonight Show* and showed Johnny Carson how well I could putt. At that time, it was almost **inevitable** that I would be a great golfer. But just how good I would get—nobody could have predicted that.

   a. certain, unavoidable
   b. unheard of, rare
   c. unlikely, slim chance of

2. I ended up going to college at Stanford University. While I was there, I obviously kept playing golf. I was **tenacious** on the golf course. No matter how bad a shot I hit, I never gave up. Grinding—that's what I call it. I always kept grinding. Anyway, I was the best amateur golfer around. I won everything, including the U.S. Amateur Championship. When I graduated Stanford, I turned pro.

   a. lackadaisical, flippant
   b. calm, cool, considered
   c. determined, keeping a firm grip on

3. Just weeks after I turned pro, I entered the Masters Golf Tournament. Whaddya know—I won. By 12 strokes—the greatest margin of victory ever in the tournament. I was only 21. I guess my dad was **clairvoyant** when he gave me my first set of clubs. I guess he knew I would become the best player in the world—maybe the best player ever.

   a. crazy, not in control of one's faculties
   b. exceptionally insightful, able to foresee the future
   c. intelligent, able to make the right decision

Who Am I?

Extra Exercise: Using three words from the glossary, describe what you know about the athlete outlined above. If you know absolutely nothing about this dude, select a different athlete.

39. The Pentagon Papers

Over 60,000 American lives and millions of Vietnamese lives were lost in the Vietnam War. The thing is, it could have been even worse, were it not for a man named Daniel Ellsberg.

Ellsberg was a professor who had access to the Pentagon Papers, a report being put together by the U.S. Defense Department in 1967. The report detailed the government's deliberate deception of the American people regarding the Vietnam War. Ellsberg, who worked on the project, had been an ardent early supporter of the U.S. role in Vietnam but, by the project's end, had become seriously opposed to U.S. involvement. He felt compelled to reveal the nature of U.S. participation there, and in 1971, leaked a copy of the report to *The New York Times*. The newspaper published it, and a country already distrustful of the government had hard proof that the war was being fought for the wrong reasons.

That was the last straw.

Public support for the war faded to almost zero, and every politician suddenly had a plan for getting the country out of the war as soon as possible.

Is there something going on in the country today that you would risk your future to stop, the way Ellsberg did to end the Vietnam War? Use the following three SAT words to describe what you think is the country's biggest problem right now.

mitigate—to soften, or make milder

procrastinate—to unnecessarily delay, postpone, put off

resilient—quick to recover, bounce back

Extra Exercise: What would you do to solve this problem? Use three words from the glossary and explain.

40. Siegfried and Roy Toy with Death by Tiger

Las Vegas has a lounge act where two guys with questionably long hair (probably extensions) and tight, glittery attire make several white lions and tigers do their bidding. Their names are *Siegfried* and *Roy*. They make millions of dollars entertaining gray-haired gamblers from every corner of the country. They've been doing it for years. And they are still alive and scratch-free.

For this exercise, you're pleading with a lion to spare your life. Use the following SAT words to come up with the following pleas. The situation provided will help guide you.

Situation: You will reward it handsomely to leave you alone.

SAT word: **remuneration**—pay or reward for work, trouble

Your plea: _____

Situation: You lavish it with praise and compliment its *feline*-ity.

SAT word: **sycophant**—self-serving flatterer, yes man

Your plea: _____

Situation: You explain that if it tries to eat you, you will kick its tiger butt from here to Africa.

SAT word: **burly**—brawny, husky

Your plea: _____

Situation: You tell them that many of your best friends are tigers, so you don't understand why it would would want to eat you.

SAT word: **adversarial**—antagonistic, competitive

Your plea: _____

Extra Exercise: Have you ever been threatened by an animal? A rabid dog? A frightening rabbit? Use three words from the glossary to explain.

41. Niagara Falls in a Barrel? You've Gotta Be Kidding

The Niagara Falls waterfall formed some 12,000 years ago at what is now the border between New York state and Canada. The volume of water flowing over the American falls is estimated at 75,000 gallons per second.

In its first 11,900 years, nobody went over the Falls on purpose—as far as we know. In the last 100 years, 15 people have attempted to ride the 170 waterfalls in a variety of contraptions, from the traditional barrel to a lashed-together amalgam of tires and fish nets. Ten intrepid fall jumpers—including the first—lived. Five others died, including the last guy, who got on a jet ski, jumped the waterfall, and tried to pull a parachute strapped to his back.

It didn't open.

Pretend your best friend has fashioned himself a barrel and is driving to the Falls tomorrow. You must talk him out of his jump using the following words:

buffoon—clown or fool

canny—smart; founded on common sense

denigrate—to slur or blacken someone's reputation

discredit—to dishonor or disgrace

_____

_____

_____

_____

Extra Exercise: Some people just can't resist wild stunts. Evil Kneivel obsessed about jumping over cars on his motorcycle. Frenchman Philippe Petit walked a tightrope suspended between the World Trade Towers in New York City. Describe a challenging but safe stunt alternative for these thrill seekers. Use five words from the glossary.

42. Before Michael Jackson Was Weird, He Was Young

Before singer-songwriter extraordinaire Michael Jackson became a surgical-mask-wearing, monkey-owning plastic surgery enthusiast, he was a pop star prodigy who had topped the charts before most kids can even tie their shoes.

How did such a talented kid turn into a billionaire recluse? Was it too much fame too soon? Not enough fiber in his diet?

Let's try to figure it out. Following are theories for Jackson's inexplicable change. Each contains an SAT word. Your job is to pick right definition for the SAT word used.

Coming from a family of nine children, Michael had to constantly **vie** for attention. It affected him. He got weird.

1. **Vie** means
    a. to compete, contend.
    b. to hate, loathe.
    c. to motivate, urge.

Sick and tired of bunking with his **sullen** brother Tito on the road, Michael learned how to cheer himself up. That's why his Neverland Ranch is filled with funny chimps and pretty birds.

2. **Sullen** means
    a. sensitive, perceptive.
    b. brooding, gloomy.
    c. dapper, well-dressed.

After penning the **score** for his backup band, Michael often felt as if he had been used. Why couldn't someone else do it? It burned him, so he started to act weird.

3. **Score** means
    a. directions home.
    b. love letter.
    c. musical composition.

Extra Exercise: Imagine you have just purchased Jackson's Neverland ranch, complete with zoo and amusement park. Write a letter to your best friend describing the place, using three words from the glossary.

43. Pac-Man: More Popular Than Flared Trousers

Let's take a trip back in time—to the late 1970s, when video games were born.

First came Pong—a tennis match you played on your TV. Then came Space Invaders, an arcade game where beeping aliens descended upon your single defending ground force, dropping bombs all the way. But the 1980s brought the game that changed it all—*Pac-Man*.

In the game, four carnivorous ghosts named *Shadow*, *Speedy*, *Bashful*, and *Pokey* try to eat a dot-munching yellow circle named Pac-Man. The object: Eat all the dots before the ghosts get you. The game was so popular when it first came out that it had a cereal, a song—even a TV show.

Following are some sentences about the classic video game. Pick out the best definition of the words used.

1. The marauding ghosts are a **baleful** presence for Pac-Man, as they are always trying to kill him.
   a. harmful, with evil intentions
   b. to bark in a prolonged way
   c. rowdy, loud, unrestrained

2. You must be **dexterous** to successfully navigate Pac-Man through the mazes.
   a. harsh-sounding, badly out of tune
   b. cranky, mean-spirited
   c. skilled physically or mentally

3. One way the **diabolical** ghosts get to Pac-Man is to bait him into a corner and then surround him.
   a. emotional, troubled
   b. fiendish, wicked
   c. understood only by a learned few

4. When playing Pac-Man, it is important not to be **fazed** by a bad move or two. You have at least three tries to complete a maze.
   a. bothered, upset
   b. gladdened, filled with joy
   c. challenged, tested

Extra Exercise: Describe your favorite electronic game using three words from the glossary.

44. Senator Barry Goldwater: Conservative Republican Legend

In 1964, a fire-breathing conservative politician won the Republican nomination for president. His name was Barry Goldwater. He lost to—actually, he was destroyed by—the Democratic nominee, Lyndon Johnson, in the general election. But his right-wing views—a strong national defense, a small government, limited social programs—became the basis for what, 20 years later, would become the Reagan Revolution.

Use the following words to write a sentence that explains each of the following sentences from Barry Goldwater's "Where I Stand" statement in 1964.

On Foreign Aid: "Although we are the wealthiest nation in the world, we cannot support all of the other nations on earth, or even most of them."

SAT word: **fecund**—fertile, fruitful, productive

Your explanation: _____

_____

On Civil Rights: "We can't pass a law that will make you like me and me like you. This has to be done between us."

SAT word: **irresolvable**—unable to be resolved

Your explanation: _____

_____

On Defense: "(I) cannot support actions which may deprive our military men of the tools needed to do their job."

SAT word: **pulverize**—destroy; to pound or crush into a powder

Your explanation: _____

_____

Extra Exercise: Pretend you are running for president. Use three words from the glossary to describe how you would make the country a better place to live.

45. Invention of Television

The Boob Tube. The Idiot Box. A couch potato's best friend.

America has had a love-hate relationship with television since it was invented in the 1920s by Vladimir Zworykin. Zworykin himself ended up hating TV because of its "trivialization of everyday life." See, he always saw his invention as a learning tool—a machine that would improve the culture—instead of the vehicle for advertising that it quickly became.

Imagine you are the high-minded Zworykin and you're trying to convince people that TV should be used for cultural expression and education, not for sheer entertainment or sales. Use the following four words for a speech you'll be giving at your local university.

mock—to deride, ridicule

pedestrian—commonplace

rail (v.)—to scold with bitter or abusive language

obsequious—overly submissive, brownnosing, fawning

_____

_____

_____

_____

_____

Extra Exercise: Take the other side and explain why Zworykin couldn't be more wrong. Use the same words.

46. Reality Television Rules

Most reality shows follow one of two tracks. First, there are the "relationship" shows like *The Bachelor* and *The Bachelorette*, *Joe Millionaire*, and all of the marrying permutations (*Married by America*, *Bridezilla*, etc.) In these shows, contestants willingly allow cameras to follow them into the most personal of romantic situations in order to find true love and/or money.

Second, there are the "extreme" shows, like *Fear Factor*, *The Mole*, and the grandfather of them all, *Survivor*. In these shows, people compete physically and mentally for lots of money. They have to do stuff like eat cockroaches, survive on deserted islands, and trick other contestants into failing.

All of these shows are popular because the people competing aren't actors, and if they are, like on *Celebrity Mole*, for instance, they aren't acting. What they're doing is real. Hence the term "reality show," even when the situations are about as unreal as you can get.

Pretend you're creating a new reality television program called *Cave Doctor*. In this show, a doctor trapped underground has to use whatever he can to operate on willing contestants. The bigger and more important the organ the contestant allows the cave doctor to remove or replace, the more money he or she gets ($50,000 for an appendix, $100,000 for a kidney, etc.)

malediction—curse
malady—disease
primeval—ancient, primitive

_____

_____

_____

_____

Extra Exercise: Can you think of a way to work dating or romance into *Cave Doctor*? Use three words from the glossary to describe your idea.

47. Saving American Farms: Farm Aid Does Its Part

Since 1985 a group of musicians has performed every year to raise money for America's family farms. Led by Willie Nelson, Neil Young, and John Mellencamp, the annual *Farm Aid* concerts draw popular rock, country, pop, and rap bands to America's hinterlands. The concerts raise millions of dollars that are used in a variety of ways to help farmers—from helping them pay off their loans to funding their lobbying efforts in Congress.

The country has all sorts of problems that would benefit from the dollars raised at benefit concerts. Imagine you are in a popular band and you'd like to have a benefit concert for your favorite cause. First pick your cause, whether it's urban poverty, cruelty to animals—or even a concert to pay for YOUR college tuition.

Next, write a paragraph asking the nearest sports stadium to donate space for one night. Using the following words, explain your cause and describe the performance that would take place.

donor—benefactor, contributor

fervid—passionate, intense

cavort—to frolic, prance about

encore—additional performance, often demanded by audience

_____

_____

_____

_____

Extra Exercise: Write an advertisement for your local newspaper advertising the event you just created. Use three words from the glossary in your ad.

48. Babe Ruth: Tough Beginnings

Perhaps the greatest home-run hitter ever to play baseball, Babe Ruth single-handedly turned around the then **hapless** New York Yankees, clobbered more home runs than anyone else in baseball, and became one of the most famous people in the world. But life didn't start out so easily for him.

At the age of seven, Ruth's parents felt they could no longer care for him, and so turned over custody of him to St. Mary's Industrial School for Boys, a Catholic reformatory in Baltimore. He lived there until he was 19, when, as a young baseball player, he was signed to a contract with the Baltimore Orioles. Ruth was a great pitcher but an even better hitter, and he eventually set a major league record for number of home runs—an unprecedented 714—until Hank Aaron **superseded** that number.

Even after he gained immeasurable fame, Ruth never forgot his hardscrabble beginnings, and spent much of his time off the field **championing** the causes of underprivileged children around the world.

1. **Hapless** means unfortunate, having bad luck. That means that when the Babe turned the Yankees around, they
    a. became much worse.
    b. became much better.
    c. stayed just about the same.

2. Define **supersede**.

    _____

3. To **champion** means
    a. to win.
    b. to defend, to support.
    c. to defeat.

Extra Exercise: Use three words from the glossary to describe your favorite sports star.

49. Testing Your Simpsons IQ

On December 17, 1989, *Simpsons Roasting on an Open Fire* aired on the Fox network. Television would never be the same. Animation, long relegated to Saturday morning cartoons, was finally legit, with the funniest show on TV. *The Simpsons*, which revolved around a zany, dysfunctional family in the small town of Springfield, became an instant cultural phenomenon. Its characters Homer, Bart, Marge, Lisa, and Maggie became international animated superstars.

Homer Simpson

Can life get any better for Homer Simpson? He juggles the roles of husband, father, Safety Inspector at the Springfield Nuclear Power Plant, bowler, beer drinker, astronaut, small business owner, and dreamer, and makes it all look easy. But it wasn't always so easy for Homer; he was at the bottom of his high-school class and managed to earn the distinction of being the longest-term entry-level employee at the power plant. With his high-school sweetheart, Marge Bouvier, Homer settled down in a nice upper-lower-middle class neighborhood to raise his three precious children. Homer is fond of Duff Beer, donuts, Marge's pork chops, and watching the Bee Guy on the Spanish channel.

Selma Bouvier

The only thing Selma Bouvier hates more than her brother-in-law, Homer, is being single. She has been married twice and divorced twice as well. First, she married Sideshow Bob after he served his prison term for framing Krusty the Clown. That marriage ended amicably after Bob tried to blow up Selma during their honeymoon. Her second marriage was to Troy McClure—Selma wanted to restore his tarnished reputation. That marriage ended, too. For now, Selma's most enduring relationship is with Jub Jub, her pet iguana.

Santa's Little Helper

Santa's Little Helper may not have been lucky for Homer Simpson at the racetrack one Christmas Eve, but he sure has turned out to be one fortunate dog. Loved and doted on by his owner, Bart Simpson, Santa's Little Helper enjoys the sort of life that most dogs only dream about: He belongs to a tolerant family that lets him tear up the furniture and eat from the table; he enjoyed a brief but fruitful relationship with a lovely greyhound; and he earned a degree from a prestigious canine academy. Of course, his life hasn't been all milkbones: His legs were accidentally broken by Mr. Burns and he was abandoned by the Simpson family for Laddie, a better-bred dog Bart bought from a catalog.

Ned Flanders

The Good Lord has been very good to Ned Flanders, thank you very much. Not only has he been blessed with his lovely wife, Maude, but together they have raised two proper little children, Rod and Todd. Ned lives in one of the best kept houses in Evergreen Terrace, and the Leftorium, his left-handed-only retail business, is booming. There isn't much for Ned to complain about. Except for his neighbor, Homer Simpson, and all of his swearing on the other side of the fence.

Following is a multiple-choice quiz that tests your knowledge of *The Simpsons*.

1. Selma has been divorced twice. If she were to marry again, it would probably be with a lot of trepidation. **Trepidation** means
   a. curiosity.
   b. inexperience.
   c. fear and anxiety.

2. Santa's Little Helper belongs to a tolerant family. **Tolerant** means
   a. hard-working.
   b. demanding.
   c. respectful, permissive.

3. Ned Flanders, the Simpsons' goody-two-shoes neighbor, is very
   a. devout.
   b. duplicitous.
   c. fortuitous.

4. Homer is a fatuous windbag who is rarely right, though he usually means well. **Fatuous** means
   a. overweight.
   b. stupid.
   c. stealthy.

Extra Exercise: Suppose you were basing a script for an animated TV show on your friends or family. Use four words from the glossary to describe each of the main characters.

50. Guess Who I Am?

1. First off, I have a freakish voice. Not bad freakish—good freakish. Six octaves at last count. That's kind of how I got discovered. I had a demo tape; a big-time music executive popped it in his car stereo one night, and voilà, I had a record contract. But there are tons of people with beautiful singing voices. I attribute my fame to **assiduously** courting mainstream pop music styles and not trying anything too, well, freaky.

   a. off-and-on
   b. precociously
   c. persistently

2. My first album did really well. In 1991 I won Best New Artist and Best Female Vocalist. That almost never happens. Still, while it might seem like I'm lucky, I have been very **diligent** in pursuing my career. I never go too long without releasing a single, I put out an album every year or two, and I fastidiously change my look to stay on top of current fashion trends. It's hard work!

   a. opportunistic
   b. aggressive, ruthless
   c. careful and hard-working

3. My life was definitely charmed, until *Glitter* came along. It was a film based on my life that I starred in—my first big break in the movies. I also recorded the soundtrack. Big mistake. The movie was awful and the record didn't sell as well as everyone had hoped. It was all too much, and I had an itty bitty breakdown. After the dust settled, I got out of my record contract and started all over again. I got to **collaborate** with producers Jimmy Jam and Jermaine Dupri on my "comeback" album, *Charmbracelet*. I also got offered more parts in more movies, so I guess *Glitter* couldn't have been that bad! Okay, I admit it, it was terrible.

   a. party all night
   b. work together
   c. debate social theory

Who Am I?

Extra Exercise: Write a paragraph describing what you know about the singer outlined above, using three words from the glossary.

51. The Legend of Bigfoot

While accounts of a large, hairy creature inhabiting the U.S.'s Pacific Northwest date back to 1884, the Bigfoot craze got its real start in 1958, when a crew was building a road through what had previously been untouched wilderness. At night, the crew's camp was repeatedly visited by a visitor that threw 50-gallon drums around the site and left huge, human-like footprints. The site manager took plaster **casts** of the footprints, the media descended, and Bigfoot was born.

While several footprint casts now exist and some fuzzy film footage of a large, **simian** creature has been taken, there is still no **definitive** evidence that Bigfoot really exists. Hoax or not, the legend of Bigfoot is very real and continues to grow each time a **vivid** close encounter is retold.

1. **Vivid** means
   a. erratic.
   b. strongly perceived.
   c. cautious.

2. **Simian** means
   a. portly, corpulent.
   b. apelike.
   c. wellread.

3. **Definitive** evidence of Bigfoot's existence would be
   a. a captured creature.
   b. a fuzzy videotape of Bigfoot in the woods.
   c. an account of a close encounter with Bigfoot.

4. Define **cast** as used above.

   _____

   _____

Extra Exercise: Do you believe that Bigfoot exists? The Loch Ness Monster? Space aliens? Use three words from the glossary to explain your reasoning.

52. Hunter S. Thompson: Gonzo Journalist

Journalism is easy. Anyone can do it.

First, you go on assignment, say, to listen to a campaign speech, to hear a candidate **opine** on a topic such as "How to save the forests." You're a journalist, so you write down what the candidate says, and what everyone there thinks about what is said. You add a few background details, such as the candidate's birthday and maybe the last job he or she held, and that's your article.

Gonzo journalism, on the other hand, requires more innovation. You still have to go on assignment, say, to listen to a campaign speech, and do all the things just mentioned. But then you have to make it interesting and insightful. Instead of mentioning the year the candidate was born, you might comment on the **proclivity** the candidate has for smacking his or her lips between sentences. Instead of mentioning his or her previous job, you make a **wry** comment that the podium being used during this **oration** about "How to save the forests" looks as though it was made from about 500 pounds of plywood. You write the truth, not just the facts.

Hunter S. Thompson invented gonzo journalism—journalism with a **jaded** point of view—in the 1960s. *Fear and Loathing in Las Vegas, Hell's Angels,* and *The Great Shark Hunt* are among his classic books.

1. To **opine** means to
   a. talk loudly.
   b. give an opinion.
   c. complain about.

2. Which of the following is a **wry** comment?
   a. It is nice out today.
   b. That makes me feel so sad.
   c. If you're the salt of the earth, I'll take some pepper.

3. Define **jaded**.

4. Define **oration**.

5. Someone with a **proclivity** for smacking his or her lips might
   a. have a dry mouth.
   b. never smack his lips.
   c. need to eat more fiber.

Extra Exercise: Using gonzo journalism, describe the last trip you took. Use five outrageous words from the glossary.

53. Sonny and Cher: The Golden Years

In 1962, Cherilyn Sarkisian—a 16-year-old girl with Hollywood dreams—met Sonny Bono, an aspiring singer and songwriter. Three years later, Sonny and Cher recorded the #1 smash hit "I Got You Babe." More hit singles and a TV variety show soon followed.

Even though they were married and happy for a time, Sonny and Cher never looked right together. She was about 6 feet tall and gorgeous. He was about 5 feet tall and had a droopy moustache and bad hair. The odd-voiced, physically mismatched couple probably did as well as was possible. They split up in the '70s, but their legend lives on.

Following are some odd-voiced, physically mismatched celebrities. Use the SAT word that is provided to describe what kind of performing act you think they would from. We'll start you off with an example.

Celebrities: Fran Drescher (The Nanny) and Bob Dylan (famous folk singer)
SAT Word: **rancor**—bitter hatred

Stage Act Description: Bob and Fran made it big in the UK with the hit single

"Nng Nng, I Love You" before rancor between the two broke out. Apparently Fran

had refused to share her nasal spray with the aging rock legend.

Celebrities: Grungy comedian Janeane Garofalo and studly actor Rob Lowe
SAT Word: **tawdry**—gaudy, cheap, showy

Stage Act Description: _____

_____

Celebrities: Actress Cameron Diaz and bat-biting metalhead Ozzy Osbourne
SAT Word: **unanimity**—state of total agreement or unity

Stage Act Description: _____

_____

Extra Exercise: Pick a singer you'd like to form a band with. Use three words from the glossary to describe what would make your act unique.

54. The Gulf War

You may wonder when all the bad blood between the United States and Iraq began. Well, in 1990, Iraq invaded its oil-rich neighbor, Kuwait. That was a bad idea.

Former U.S. President George Bush quickly put together a coalition of countries that ordered Iraq to withdraw from Kuwait. When Iraqi President Saddam Hussein irreverently refused to do so, the United States and its allies attacked. 530,000 troops stormed Kuwait, forcing the Iraqis out and inflicting massive devastation on their army.

General Norman Schwarzkopf was in charge of the invasion, called "Desert Storm." As he said at the time, "Any soldier worth his salt should be antiwar. And still there are things worth fighting for."

Pretend you were the general in charge of the troops at the time. Use the following four words to write an inspirational speech for them. We'll get you started.

insidious—sly, treacherous, devious

deleterious—harmful, destructive, detrimental

pernicious—very harmful

Men! Women! Today is the day you must fight for the most important thing in the

world—your country!

_____

_____

_____

_____

Extra Exercise: The invasion of Iraq was called "Desert Storm." Make up three other names for that war using three different words from the glossary.

55. The 1950s: Conformity Is Good

After World War II, the United States could finally relax. Millions of soldiers came home, got married, had kids, and settled down. After years of "doing without" in order to supply the war effort, Americans lavished money on themselves, and bought cookie-cutter homes in identical suburbs across the nation. They also bought big cars, bought big appliances, and got hooked on a brand-new invention—the television.

Pretend you are the first family to move into a brand-spanking-new suburb and it is your job to attract other people to your little slice of heaven. Write the text for an advertisement in your local paper using the following three words. Explain how the American Dream is alive and well, right here, at Pine Terrace Manor Estates, where you and your family live in an aluminum-sided, three-bedroom house on a man-made pond full of 7-inch bluegill.

conformist—person who complies with accepted rules and customs

divergent—separating, moving in different directions from a particular point

emulate—to imitate; follow an example

Come Join Us at
Pine Terrace Manor Estates

_____

_____

_____

_____

_____

Extra Exercise: Suburbs were built after World War II to house all of the returning GIs and their families. Would you prefer to live in the suburbs, a city, or out in the country? Use at least three words from the glossary to explain.

56. The 1960s: Lots of Newfangled Changes

The sixties were about more than just free love, Volkswagen Beetles, and bad acid. As President John F. Kennedy said in his inaugural address in 1960, the "torch has been passed to a new generation of Americans." That generation—people born during and after World War II, the largest single generation ever in America—did a lot to define the decade, and to influence America to this day.

Perhaps the most defining accomplishment of the 1960s was the Civil Rights Act of 1964, which banned segregation and discrimination in places like restaurants, hotels, and movie theaters. "Whites Only" signs across the nation were taken down, although not without a struggle. Thousands of people were beaten and killed as the nation struggled to free itself from institutional racism.

Imagine that you are mayor of your town, and that the Civil Rights Act has just become law. Write a speech explaining how the Act will affect the citizens in your town. Include the following three words.

amicable—friendly, agreeable

antagonist—foe, opponent, adversary

circuitous—indirect, taking the longest route

_____

_____

_____

_____

Extra Exercise: As part of your speech, explain how the Civil Rights Act was such a breakthrough for society. Use three words from the glossary.

57. The 1970s: The Scary and Addled Decade

How does one wrap up a decade like the 1970s?

It started with a president (Richard Nixon) resigning from office—the first one ever to do so. Then the Vietnam War ended (hurray!). Then a peanut farmer (Jimmy Carter) was elected president (seemed like a good idea, I guess), there was a nationwide oil shortage, a bunch of Americans were taken hostage in Iran, and Disco came and went.

Oh yeah, and New York City went broke and had to be bailed out by Congress, the Chrysler car corporation went broke and had to be bailed out by Congress, Three Mile Island Nuclear Power Plant in Pennsylvania had a meltdown. . . . Did I mention Disco?

Pretend your car is number 234 in a gas line at your local filling station (the 1970s oil shortages caused gas lines that snaked for blocks). Your neighbor's car is number 235. Tell him what you think of the seventies using the following four words. We'll get you started.

denounce—to accuse, blame

detrimental—causing harm or injury

enervating—weakening; tiring

fraught—full of, accompanied by

Hey Tom, nice flared pants! Can you believe this line? _____

_____

_____

_____

_____

Extra Exercise: Using three words from the glossary, describe something current that you believe originated in the 1970s.

58. The 1980s: The Greed Decade

The decade of the eighties is remembered for the grandfatherly presence of President Ronald Reagan, the beginning of the AIDS epidemic, heavy metal hair bands like Mötley Crüe—and greed.

While the country was falling further and further into debt, a group of high-flying Wall Street financiers was surreptitiously making enormous profits by buying stock in companies that were about to merge with other companies. Once those mergers took place, the companys' stock values shot up, thereby turning those individuals into multimillionaires.

The thing was, they cheated. Using "insider information" to their advantage, they made billions of dollars for themselves and their friends. That is, until of the FBI caught up with them. The most notable of these men was Michael Milken, who was convicted of fraud and ended up in the slammer.

What if you were a high-flying Wall Street financier who had broken the law for your own financial gain? Write a letter to the FBI explaining why you did it. Use the following four words. We'll get you started.

parsimony—stinginess

spurious—lacking authenticity; counterfeit, false

predicament—difficult situation

profuse—lavish, extravagant

Dear, Kind, Sweet Mr. FBI Man, I can explain everything. _____

_____

_____

_____

_____

Extra Exercise: You have just spent three years in prison. Using three words from the glossary, write a letter to the parole board explaining how you have learned your lesson and will never cheat again.

59. The 1990s: The Boom Decade

The decade of the nineties started off shaky. Unemployment was up, we were fighting a war with Iraq, and "Members Only" jackets were still popular. That all changed seemingly with the election of Bill Clinton. All of a sudden, unemployment dropped like a stone, the stock market started roaring, the Internet made billionaires out of people barely out of college—and the only "Members Only" jackets you could find were in thrift shop windows. Once 2000 came around, the boom turned into a bust, and unemployment lines snaked around the block, but it sure was fun while it lasted!

Use the following words about optimism and success to describe some of the good things that happened to you in the 1990s. We'll get you started.

exemplary—outstanding, an example to others

fortuitous—happening by luck, fortunate

opulent—wealthy

What a grand and wonderful decade! There are so many good things that happened,

it is hard for me to know where to start.

_____

_____

_____

_____

Extra Exercise: Not everything went so well in the 1990s. The president was impeached and a white supremacist bombed the federal building in Oklahoma City. Use three words from the glossary to descibe an event you remember about that time.

60. Ben Franklin: Kind and Gentle Inventor

You probably know Ben Franklin as one of those Revolutionary War rabble-rousers, wearing wigs, signing declarations of independence, treating England with **disdain**, traveling to France a lot—a true **iconoclast**. What you may not know is that our **compatriot** invented things and coined the **dictum**, "Well done is better."

Franklin's **incisive** imagination brought many a **boon** to our country—and the world: He invented all kinds of cool gadgets that met the needs of many people. For instance, he had poor eyesight, so he invented bifocals. Ships in that crazy era were always getting hit by lightning, so he invented the lighting rod to help protect them.

Speaking of protecting people, Ben was so fed up with colonial houses going up in smoke because of dangerous fireplaces that he thought up the Franklin stove, a cast iron jobber that heated the house and cooked the food. When, in retirement, Ben turned to reading as his favorite pastime, he invented the "long arm," a stick with a claw on the end of it, so he could reach the books highest on his shelves.

1. Define **compatriot**.

   _____

2. What does **boon** mean?
   a. something to be thankful for
   b. something to be angry about
   c. something to brag about

3. Define **incisive**.

   _____

4. Define **dictum**.

   _____

5. Who would you call an **iconoclast** and why?

   _____

6. Define **disdain**.

   _____

Extra Exercise: Describe a wacky invention, such as a portable pet potty, a car bib, or a head-mounting umbrella. Use five words from the glossary.

61. Guess Who I Am?

1. The first year I played baseball in the major leagues, my team made it to the playoffs. It was great—we hadn't been to the playoffs in over ten years. Once we made it in, we won the first two games, but then we suffered a series of **calamitous** events. Bad pitching, no hitting, bad fielding, bad umpires—you name it, it happened. We lost three in a row and our season was over.

   a. beneficial, pleasing
   b. disastrous, catastrophic
   c. weird, unexpected

2. My second year in baseball, I came into my own. No longer was I the **precocious** shortstop on a team full of veteran stars—I was fast becoming a star in my own right. People were comparing me to the best players in the game. That year, my team won the World Series. And it was just the beginning.

   a. annoying, grating
   b. well-rounded, educated
   c. unusually advanced at an early age

3. In three of my first five years in the major leagues, my team won the World Series. And I was the major reason for it. I got a shoe contract. I got a cereal named after me. I got on the cover of *GQ* magazine. I had famous girlfriends. I might be the luckiest guy in the world, and believe me, I **relish** every day I am on this planet. Life is great.

   a. feel sad about, worry about
   b. enjoy greatly
   c. talk about, discuss

Who Am I?

Extra Exercise: Write a paragraph about what you know about the athlete described above, using three words from the glossary.

Answer Key

1. **Gap-Toothed and Proud of It**
   1. c
   2. b
   3. c

2. **Billie Jean King: One Giant Leap**
   N/A

3. **Jimmy Hoffa Never Made it Home to Grill His Meat**
   N/A

4. **Impeaching a President: What Happened**
   1. Infamous means famous for having committed bad deeds.
   2. A euphemism is an inoffensive word/phrase that is used in place of a more distasteful one.
   3. b
   4. a
   5. To impeach means to charge with misdeeds in public office.

5. **Guess Who I Am?**
   1. b
   2. a
   3. c
   I am Serena Williams.

6. **Woodstock '69: The Original**
   1. a
   2. c
   3. c

7. **Christina Applegate: Making It in Hollywood**
   N/A

8. **Junior Johnson: Stock Car Hero**
   N/A

9. **Carol Burnett: Ear-Tugging Comedienne**
   N/A

10. **Guess Who I Am?**
    1. c
    2. a
    3. c
    I am Arnold Schwarzenegger.

11. **William Randolph Hearst: Big Man Media**
    N/A

12. Soccer Boogie

1. a
2. b
3. a
4. c
5. a

13. Herbert Hoover Wasn't Such a Bad Guy Really

N/A

14. Guess Who I Am?

I am Beck.

15. Wisconsin: Got Milk?

1. a
2. c
3. a
4. c

16. 1968: Riots in Chicago

N/A

17. Tom Hanks: He Used to Wear a Dress

N/A

18. Jesse Ventura: From Wrassler to Governor

1. a
2. To fell means to cut down.
3. c
4. b

19. The Hives: Perfect Punks

N/A

20. Guess Who I Am?

1. c
2. a
3. a
I am Howard Stern.

21. Brad Pitt: His Love Life

N/A

22. Jackie Chan: Star in Asia, Cult Hero in America

N/A

23. Guess Who I Am?

1. a
2. c
3. a
I am Jim Carrey.

24. Lost Generation Is Found

N/A

25. Guess Who I Am?
1. b
2. c
3. c
I am John F. Kennedy.

26. Apollo 11: Eagle's Tricky Landing
1. To hasten means to hurry, to speed up.
2. c
3. b
4. Grasped means perceived and understood.

27. Friends: No One Told You Life Would Be This Way
1. c
2. a
3. c
4. b
5. a
6. c

28. The Guggenheim Museum
1. b
2. b
3. a
4. c

29. The Great Communicator
N/A

30. Buckaroo Bonzai: A Cowboy's Gotta Live
N/A

31. Watergate: More Than Just a Presidential Scandal
N/A

32. Guess Who I Am?
1. a
2. c
3. b
I am Harrison Ford.

33. Hot Dog Jungle
N/A

34. Andy Warhol: Soup Cans . . . and So Much More
N/A

35. Reverend Jesse Jackson: A Life of Service
1. a
2. c
3. Munificent means generous.
4. c

36. Mae West Was the Best

N/A

37. Lockdown USA: Prison Overcrowding

N/A

38. Guess Who I Am?

1. a
2. c
3. b
I am Tiger Woods.

39. The Pentagon Papers

N/A

40. Siegfried and Roy Toy with Death by Tiger

N/A

41. Niagara Falls in a Barrel? You've Gotta Be Kidding

N/A

42. Before Michael Jackson Was Weird, He Was Young

1. a
2. b
3. c

43. Pac-Man: More Popular Than Flared Trousers

1. a
2. c
3. b
4. a

44. Senator Barry Goldwater: Conservative Republican Legend

N/A

45. Invention of Television

N/A

46. Reality Television Rules

N/A

47. Saving American Farms: Farm Aid Does Its Part

N/A

48. Babe Ruth: Tough Beginnings

1. b
2. Supersede means to take the place of; to replace.
3. b

49. Testing Your Simpsons IQ

1. c
2. c
3. a
4. b

50. Guess Who I Am?

1. c
2. c
3. b

I am Mariah Carey.

51. The Legend of Bigfoot

1. b
2. b
3. a
4. A cast is a copy or replica.

52. Hunter S. Thompson: Gonzo Journalist

1. b
2. c
3. Jaded means tired by excess or overuse.
4. An oration is a lecture or formal speech.
5. a

53. Sonny and Cher: The Golden Years

N/A

54. The Gulf War

N/A

55. The 1950s: Conformity is Good

N/A

56. The 1960s: Lots of Newfangled Changes

N/A

57. The 1970s: The Scary and Addled Decade

N/A

58. The 1980s: The Greed Decade

N/A

59. The 1990s: The Boom Decade

N/A

60. Ben Franklin: Kind and Gentle Inventor

1. A compatriot is a fellow countryman.
2. a
3. Incisive means perceptive, penetrating.
4. A dictum is an authoritative statement; a popular saying.
5. An iconoclast is one who attacks traditional beliefs. Answers will vary.
6. Disdain means a feeling of scorn or contempt.

61. Guess Who I Am?

1. b
2. c
3. b

I am Derek Jeter, shortstop for the New York Yankees.

Glossary

SAT Vocabulary Study Aids

No one can predict exactly which words will show up on your SAT test, but there are certain words that the test makers favor. The more of these you know, the better. The following word list contains typical SAT words with example sentences. The more you become comfortable with them, the more you'll reduce your anxiety about the test.

Memorizing SAT Words

The very best way to improve your vocabulary is to read. Choose challenging, college-level material. If you encounter an unknown word, put it on a flashcard or in your vocabulary notebook.

Here's a three-step method for helping you with memorization:

1. Memorize ten new words a day, using one or more of the techniques below.

2. Reinforce what you've learned. Periodically quiz yourself on all the words you've learned so far.

3. Two weeks before the test, stop learning new words. Spend a week reviewing the word list. Rest up during the last week.

Techniques for Memorizing Words

- Learn words in groups. You can group words by a common root or by related meaning.

- Use flashcards. Write down new words or word groups and run through them when you have a few minutes to spare. Put one new word or word group on one side of an index card and put a short definition(s) on the back.

- Keep a vocabulary notebook. List words in one column and their definitions in another. Test yourself. Cover up the meanings, and see which words you can define from memory. Make a sample sentence using each word in context.

- Think of hooks that lodge a new word in your mind—create visual images of words.

- Use rhymes, pictures, songs, and any other devices that help you remember words.

A

■ ABANDON (n.)—total lack of inhibition
With her strict parents gone, Kelly danced all night with abandon.

■ ABHOR—to loathe, detest
After she failed repeatedly to learn the Pythagorean theorem, Susan began to abhor geometry.

■ ABRIDGE—to condense, shorten
The teacher assigned an abridged version of *Tristram Shandy* to her class, as the original was very long.

■ ABSCOND—to depart secretly
After being fired, the disgruntled worker absconded in the middle of the night with six computers.

■ ABSTEMIOUS—sparing or limited in appetite, restrictive
His abstemious diet helped to keep him slim.

■ ACCOLADE—praise, distinction
The winner of the spelling bee beamed as accolades were heaped upon her.

■ ACCRETION—growth in size or increase in amount
The committee's fundraising efforts resulted in an accretion in scholarship money.

■ ACME—highest point; summit
The dictator was assassinated just as he reached the acme of his power.

■ ACQUITTAL—release from blame
The public was astonished at the jury's acquittal of the serial killer—how could they let him go?

■ ACRIMONIOUS—bitter, filled with animosity
The couple's acrimonious divorce made their mutual friends feel uncomfortable.

■ ADAGE—old saying or proverb
"A penny saved is a penny earned" is a popular adage.

■ ADAPT—to accommodate; adjust
Although it may be difficult at first, we all have to adapt to the new computer system.

■ ADDLED—muddled, confused
Walking through the desert for so long addled his mind.

■ ADHERE—to cling or follow without deviation
He was a strict Catholic who adhered to all the teachings of the Church.

■ ADROIT—skillful, accomplished, highly competent
The adroit athlete completed even the most difficult obstacle course with ease.

■ ADULATION—high praise
After Ana's piano recital, the audience lavished her with adulation.

■ ADVERSARIAL—antagonistic, competitive
The brothers' adversarial relationship made it impossible for them to support each other in times of need.

■ ADVERSITY—difficult or harmful situation
She has faced a lot of adversity throughout her childhood.

■ AESTHETIC—pertaining to beauty or art
The museum curator, with her fine aesthetic sense, created an exhibit that was a joy to behold.

■ AFFABLE—friendly, easy to approach
The affable postman was on good terms with those on his route.

■ AFFECTED (adj.)—pretentious, phony
The affected hairdresser spouted French phrases, though she had never been to France.

■ AFFINITY—fondness, liking; similarity
Jorge felt an instant affinity for his new neighbor when he learned that he, too, was a Broncos fan.

■ AFFRONT (n.)—personal offense, insult
Clyde took the waiter's insulting remark as an affront to his whole family.

■ ALACRITY—cheerful willingness, eagerness; speed
The eager dog fetched with alacrity the stick that had been tossed for him.

■ ALLAY—to lessen, ease, or soothe
The nurse tried to allay the couple's fears that their son's health had deteriorated.

■ ALLEVIATE—to relieve, improve partially
This medicine will help to alleviate the pain.

■ ALLUSION—indirect reference
He was sometimes referred to as "the Slugger," an allusion to his ability to hit the baseball very hard.

■ AMALGAM—mixture, combination, alloy
Her character is an unusual amalgam of contradictory traits.

■ AMELIORATE—to make better, improve
Conditions in the hospital were ameliorated by the hiring of dozens of expertly trained nurses.

■ AMICABLE—friendly, agreeable
Despite their former arguments, the team was able to form an amicable working relationship.

■ AMPLE—abundant, plentiful
Though our backpacks were small, we had ample food for the hike.

■ ANACHRONISM—something chronologically inappropriate
The aged hippie used anachronisms like "groovy" and "far out" that had not been popular for years.

■ ANATHEMA—ban, curse; something shunned or disliked
Sweaty, soiled clothing was anathema to the elegant Madeleine.

■ ANCILLARY—accessory; subordinate; helping
Reforms were instituted at the main factory, but not at its ancillary plants, so defects continued to occur.

■ ANIMOSITY—hatred, hostility
The deep—rooted animosity between them made it difficult for the cousins to work together.

■ ANTAGONIST—foe, opponent, adversary
The politicians became bitter antagonists during the drawn-out campaign.

■ ANTIPATHY—dislike, hostility; extreme opposition or aversion
The antipathy between the French and the English regularly erupted into open warfare.

■ ANTITHESIS—exact opposite or direct contrast
The ill-mannered boy was often described as the antithesis of his sweet sister.

■ APATHY—lack of feeling or emotion
The apathy of voters is so great that less than half of those eligible to vote bother to do so.

■ APHORISM—old saying or pithy statement
The country doctor was given to aphorisms such as "Still waters run deep."

■ APOCRYPHAL—not genuine; fictional
Sharon suspected that the story about alligators in the sewer was apocryphal.

■ APPEASE—to satisfy, placate, calm, pacify
We all sang lullabies to try to appease the bawling infant.

■ APPROPRIATE (v.)—to take possession of
Lucia came up with the great idea to appropriate the abandoned building for storage.

■ ARCANE—secret, obscure, known only to a few
The arcane rituals of the sect were passed down through many generations.

■ ARDENT—passionate, enthusiastic, fervent
After losing 25 games straight, even the Mets' most ardent fans realized the team wouldn't finish first.

■ ARDUOUS—extremely difficult, laborious
Amy thought she would pass out after completing the arduous climb up the mountain.

■ ARTICULATE (adj.)—well spoken, expressing oneself clearly
She is such an articulate defender of labor that unions are among her strongest supporters.

■ ARTISAN—craftsperson; expert
Artisans were among the most valued citizens of the kingdom for their skills in tool-making.

■ ASCERTAIN—to determine, discover, make certain of
Try as he might, the archaeologist couldn't ascertain the correct age of the Piltdown man's skeleton.

■ ASPERSION—false rumor, damaging report, slander
It is unfair to cast aspersions on someone behind his or her back.

■ ASPIRE—to have great hopes; to aim at a goal
Although Sid started out in the mailroom, he aspired to owning the company someday.

■ ASSIDUOUS—diligent, persistent, hard-working
The chauffeur scrubbed the limousine assiduously, hoping to make a good impression on his employer.

■ ASSUAGE—to make less severe, ease, relieve
Like many people, Philip Larkin used alcohol to assuage his sense of meaninglessness and despair.

■ ASYMMETRICAL—not corresponding in size, shape, position
The hairstylist was shocked to find that the two sides of his customer's hair were asymmetrical.

■ AUDACIOUS—bold, daring, fearless
"And you, your majesty, may kiss my bum!" replied the audacious peasant.

■ AUGUST (adj.)—dignified, awe inspiring, venerable
The august view of the summit of the Grand Teton filled the climbers with awe.

■ AUSPICIOUS—having favorable prospects, promising
Tamika thought that having lunch with the boss was an auspicious start to her new job.

■ AVARICE—greed
Rebecca's avarice motivated her to stuff the $100 bill in her pocket instead of returning it to the man who had dropped it.

■ AVENGE—to retaliate, take revenge for an injury or crime
"You'll regret humiliating me! Someday, I will avenge this insult!" shouted the furious Count.

■ AVERSION—intense dislike
Laura took an instant aversion to Mike because of his obnoxious personality.

■ AVIARY—large enclosure housing birds
The tourists brought their cameras to the city's famous aviary, hoping to capture its exotic birds on film.

B

■ BALEFUL—harmful, with evil intentions
The sullen teenager gave his nagging mother a baleful look.

■ BALK—to refuse, stop short; prevent
The horse balked at jumping over the high fence and instead threw his rider off.

■ BANAL—trite, overly common
He used banal phrases like "Have a nice day" or "Another day, another dollar."

■ BANTER—playful conversation
Their cheerful banter helped put them at ease in the formal environment.

■ BEGUILE—to deceive, mislead; charm
Beguiled by the songs of the Sirens, Odysseus wanted to abandon all his men and forget his family.

■ BEHEMOTH—huge creature
Titanic's budget became such a behemoth that observers predicted that the film would never make a profit.

■ BELLIGERENT—hostile, tending to fight
The bartender realized that it would be fruitless to try to subdue the belligerent drunk by himself.

■ BENEFACTOR—someone giving aid or money
A mysterious benefactor paid off all Robin's bills, making it possible for her to send her children to college.

■ BENEFICENT—kindly, charitable; doing good deeds; producing good effects
Despite his tough reputation, Kirk was a beneficent man, donating millions of dollars to worthy charities.

■ BENEVOLENT—friendly and helpful
Ben and Eve volunteer at the shelter; they enjoy helping others with their benevolent acts.

■ BERATE—to scold harshly
Andy was embarrassed when his mother berated him in public for smashing the family car.

■ BESTOW—to give as a gift
The students bestowed gifts upon the teacher, attempting to procure better grades.

■ BIPED—two-footed animal
Human beings are bipeds, whereas horses are quadrupeds.

■ BLANDISH—to coax with flattery
We blandished the bouncer with compliments until he finally let us into the club.

■ BLATANT—glaring, obvious, showy
His blatant comments about their friendship embarrassed Joe's friend.

■ BOMBASTIC—using high-sounding but meaningless language
Mussolini's speeches were mostly bombastic; his boasting and outrageous claims had no basis in fact.

■ BONHOMIE—good-natured geniality; atmosphere of good cheer
The general bonhomie that characterized the party made it a joy to attend.

■ BOON—blessing, something to be thankful for
Dirk realized that his new colleague's computer skills would be a real boon to the company.

■ BUFFOON—clown or fool
The boy was known as the school buffoon, so he wasn't taken seriously as a candidate for class president.

■ BURLY—brawny, husky
Freddy was a bit intimidated by the tall, burly man standing by the bar.

■ BUTTRESS (n.)—to reinforce or support
The construction workers attempted to buttress the ceiling with pillars.

C

■ CACOPHONY—jarring, unpleasant noise
The musicians created an almost unbearable cacophony as they tuned their instruments.

■ CAJOLE—to flatter, coax, persuade
The spoiled girl could cajole her father into buying her anything.

■ CALAMITOUS—disastrous, catastrophic
Everyone hoped this year's event would be less calamitous than last year's fiasco.

■ CALUMNY—false and malicious accusation, misrepresentation, slander
The unscrupulous politician used calumny to bring down his opponent in the senatorial race.

■ CANNY—smart; founded on common sense
The executive's canny business sense saved the company from bankruptcy.

■ CAPACIOUS—large, roomy; extensive
We wondered how many hundreds of stores occupied the capacious mall.

■ CAPITULATE—to submit completely, surrender
After atom bombs devastated Hiroshima and Nagasaki, the Japanese had little choice but to capitulate.

■ CAPRICIOUS—impulsive, whimsical, without much thought
Queen Elizabeth I was quite capricious; her courtiers could never be sure who would catch her fancy.

■ CAST (n.)—copy, replica
The proud parents made a cast of their infant's first pair of shoes.

■ CAST (v.)—to fling, to throw
Embarrassed, the fisherman cast his empty line back into the water.

■ CASTIGATE—to punish, chastise, criticize severely
Authorities in Singapore harshly castigate perpetrators for what might be considered minor crimes in the United States.

■ CAULK—to make watertight
As a precaution, the sailors caulked the ship's windows with fiberglass.

■ CAUSTIC—biting, sarcastic; able to burn
Dorothy Parker gained her reputation for caustic wit from her cutting, yet clever, insults.

■ CAVORT—to frolic, prance about
The puppies looked adorable as they cavorted in the grass.

■ CELEBRITY—fame, widespread acclaim; a famous person
Once their personal lives become public, some stars have found that the price of celebrity is too high.

■ CENSORIOUS—severely critical
Saddam, unconcerned by the censorious attitude of the United Nations, continued his nuclear weapons testing.

■ CESSATION—temporary or complete halt
The cessation of hostilities ensured that soldiers were able to spend the holidays with their families.

■ CHAMPION (v.)—to defend or support
Ursula continued to champion the rights of the prisoner, even after it was proven beyond a doubt that he was guilty.

■ CHARLATAN—quack, fake
"That charlatan of a doctor prescribed the wrong medicine for me!" complained the patient.

■ CHARY—watchful, cautious, extremely shy
Mindful of the fate of the Titanic, the captain was chary of navigating the iceberg-filled sea.

■ CHERUBIC—sweet, innocent, resembling a cherub angel
Her cherubic appearance made people think her personality was also sweet, when the opposite was true.

■ CHICANERY—trickery, fraud, deception
Dishonest used-car salesmen often use chicanery to sell their beat-up old cars.

■ CHIDE—to scold, express disapproval
Florence chided her poodle for eating the birthday cake she had baked for her friend.

■ CHIMERICAL—fanciful, imaginary, visionary, impossible
The inventor's plans seemed chimerical to the conservative businessman from whom he was asking for financial support.

■ CHOLERIC—easily angered, short-tempered
The choleric principal raged at the students who had come late to school.

■ CHOICE (adj.)—specially selected, preferred
Wendell took the choicest cut of beef for himself, annoying the others at the dinner.

■ CHROMATIC—relating to color
Because he was color blind, his chromatic senses were different from those of other people.

■ CIRCUITOUS—roundabout
The cab driver took a circuitous route to the airport, making me miss my plane.

■ CIRCUMLOCUTION—roundabout, lengthy way of saying something
He avoided discussing the real issues with endless circumlocutions.

■ CIRCUMSPECT—cautious, wary
His failures have made Jack far more circumspect in his exploits than he used to be.

■ CLAIRVOYANT (adj.)—having ESP, psychic
The clairvoyant fortuneteller claimed to have communicated with the ghost of Abraham Lincoln.

■ CLANDESTINE—secretive, concealed for a darker purpose
The intern paid many clandestine visits to the president's office in the dead of night.

■ CLEMENCY—merciful leniency
Kyle begged for clemency, explaining that he had been under the influence of hallucinogens when he killed his mother.

■ CLOISTER (v.)—to confine, seclude
The Montagues cloistered their wayward daughter in a convent, hoping to keep her out of trouble.

■ COALESCE—to grow together or cause to unite as one
The different factions of the organization coalesced to form one united front against their opponents.

■ COGENT—logically forceful, compelling, convincing
Swayed by the cogent argument of the defense, the jury had no choice but to acquit the defendant.

■ COHABIT—to live together
The couple cohabited for years before finally deciding to get married.

■ COHERENT—intelligible, lucid, understandable
Cathy was so tired that her speech was barely coherent.

■ COLLABORATE—to cooperate, work together
Several students collaborated on the project.

■ COLLOQUIAL—characteristic of informal speech
The book was written in a colloquial style so that the information in it would be more user-friendly.

■ COMPATRIOT—fellow countryman
Halfway across the world from home, Jeff felt most comfortable in the company of his compatriots.

■ COMPELLING (adj.)—having a powerful and irresistible effect
The defense lawyer's compelling arguments made the jurors sympathize with the cold-blooded killer.

■ COMPLACENT—self-satisfied, smug
Philip smiled complacently as he was showered with compliments for his handling of the Buckman deal.

■ COMPLICITY—knowing partnership in wrongdoing
The two boys exchanged a look of sly complicity when their father shouted "Who broke the window?"

■ COMPRESS—to reduce, squeeze
The campers compressed the six-man tent into a tiny package.

■ CONDONE—to pardon or forgive; overlook, justify, or excuse a fault
"We cannot condone your behavior," said Raj's parents after he missed his curfew. "You're grounded."

■ CONFLAGRATION—big, destructive fire
After the conflagration had finally died down, the city center was nothing but a mass of blackened embers.

■ CONFORMIST—one who unquestionably follows the rules or customs of others
He proved himself to be a conformist on all of the issues.

■ CONFOUND—to baffle, perplex
Vince, confounded by the difficult algebra problems, threw his math book at the wall in frustration.

■ CONGENIAL—similar in tastes and habits
Couples with congenial personalities stay together longer than couples who are polar opposites.

■ CONGRUITY—correspondence, harmony, agreement
There was an obvious congruity between Mark's pleasant personality and his kind actions towards others.

■ CONJECTURE—speculation, prediction
The actor refused to comment, forcing gossip columnists to make conjectures on his love life.

■ CONSTRUE—to explain or interpret
"I wasn't sure how to construe that last remark he made," said Delia, "but I suspect it was an insult."

■ CONUNDRUM—riddle, puzzle or problem with no solution
The old man puzzled over the conundrum for hours, but eventually gave up in disgust.

■ CONVENTIONAL—typical, customary, commonplace
Conventional wisdom today says that a good job requires a college education.

■ CONVIVIAL—sociable; fond of eating, drinking, and people
The restaurant's convivial atmosphere contrasted starkly with the gloom of Maureen's empty apartment.

■ COQUETTE—woman who flirts
The coquette broke the hearts of both men at the party.

■ CORPOREAL—having to do with the body; tangible, material
Makiko realized that the "ghost" was in fact corporeal when it bumped into a chair.

■ COSMETIC (adj.)—relating to beauty; affecting the surface of something
Cosmetic surgery is generally not covered by insurance.

■ COUNTERVAIL—to counteract, to exert force against
The guerrillas countervailed the army offensive by hiding in the jungle and targeting the soldiers one by one.

■ COVERT—hidden; secret
Spies typically engage in covert operations.

■ COVET—to desire strongly something possessed by another
Harold coveted his neighbor's new car.

■ CRAVEN—cowardly
The craven lion cringed in the corner of his cage, terrified of the mouse.

■ CREDULOUS—gullible, trusting
Although some four-year-olds believe in the Easter Bunny, only the most credulous nine-year-olds do.

■ CRESCENDO—gradual increase in volume of sound
The crescendo of tension became unbearable as Evel Knievel prepared to jump his motorcycle over the school buses.

■ CULPABLE—guilty, responsible for wrong
The CEO is culpable for the bankruptcy of the company; he was, after all, in charge of it.

■ CUPIDITY—greed
The poverty—stricken man stared at the shining jewels with cupidity in his gleaming eyes.

■ CURMUDGEON—cranky person
The old man was a notorious curmudgeon who snapped at anyone who disturbed him for any reason.

D

■ DEARTH—lack, scarcity, insufficiency
The dearth of supplies in our city made it difficult to hold out for long against the attack of the aliens.

■ DEBAUCH—to corrupt, seduce from virtue or duty; indulge
After the unscrupulous count debauched the innocent girl, she was shunned by her fellow villagers.

■ DEBUNK—to discredit, disprove
It was the teacher's mission in life to debunk the myth that girls are bad at math.

■ DECIDUOUS—losing leaves in the fall; short-lived, temporary
Deciduous trees are bare in winter, which is why evergreens are used as Christmas trees.

■ DECOROUS—proper, tasteful, socially correct
The countess trained her daughters in the finer points of decorous behavior, hoping they would make a good impression when she presented them at Court.

■ DEFERENTIAL—respectful and polite in a submissive way
The respectful young law clerk treated the Supreme Court justice very deferentially.

■ DEFINITIVE—clear-cut, explicit or decisive
The brilliant 1949 production has been hailed as the definitive version of *A Doll's House*.

■ DELETERIOUS—harmful, destructive, detrimental
If we put these defective clocks on the market, it could be quite deleterious to our reputation.

■ DEMAGOGUE—leader, rabble rouser, usually appealing to emotion or prejudice
Hitler began his political career as an demagogue, giving fiery speeches in the beerhalls of Munich.

■ DENIGRATE—to slur or blacken someone's reputation
The people still loved the president, despite his enemies' attempts to denigrate his character.

■ DENOUNCE—to accuse, blame
After Stella denounced her coworkers for stealing paper clips from the office, she was promoted.

■ DENUNCIATION—public condemnation
The church staged a public denunciation of Galileo for his controversial beliefs.

■ DEPLETE—to use up, exhaust
The ozone layer is gradually being depleted by pollution.

■ DEPRAVITY—sinfulness, moral corruption
The depravity of the actor's Hollywood lifestyle shocked his traditional parents.

■ DERIDE—to mock, ridicule, make fun of
The awkward child was often derided by his "cooler" peers.

■ DESECRATE—to abuse something sacred
The archaeologist tried to explain to the explorer that he had desecrated the temple by spitting in it, but to no avail.

■ DESULTORY—at random, rambling, unmethodical
Diane had a desultory academic record; she had changed majors eight times in 3 years.

■ DETER—to discourage; prevent from happening
Some sociologists claim that the death penalty does not really deter criminals from committing crimes.

■ DETRIMENTAL—causing harm or injury
It is generally acknowledged that cigarette smoking can be detrimental to your health.

■ DEXTEROUS—skilled physically or mentally
The gymnast who won the contest was far more dexterous than the other competitors.

■ DIABOLICAL—fiendish; wicked
Sherlock Holmes's arch enemy is the diabolical Professor Moriarty.

■ DICTUM—authoritative statement; popular saying
Chris tried to live his life in accordance with the dictum "Two wrongs don't make a right."

■ DILIGENT—careful and hard-working
Because she was so diligent, she was the designated leader of the group project.

■ DIMINUTIVE—small
Napoleon made up for his diminutive stature with his aggressive personality, terrifying his courtiers.

■ DISCREDIT—to dishonor or disgrace
The war hero was discredited after it was revealed that he had fled in terror from the scene of the battle.

■ DISDAIN—to regard with scorn and contempt
The gorgeous contestant disdained her competitors, certain that she would win the Miss America crown.

■ DISPARAGE—to belittle, speak disrespectfully about
Gregorio loved to disparage his brother's dancing skills, pointing out every mistake he made on the floor.

■ DISSEMINATE—to spread far and wide
The wire service disseminates information so rapidly that events get reported shortly after they happen.

■ DISSIPATE—to scatter; to pursue pleasure to excess
The fog gradually dissipated, revealing all the ships docked in the harbor.

■ DISSONANT—harsh and unpleasant sounding
The screeching of the opera singer was completely dissonant to the ears of her audience.

■ DISSUADE—to persuade someone to alter original intentions
I tried to dissuade him from climbing Everest without an oxygen tank, but he refused to listen.

■ DITHER—to move or act confusedly or without clear purpose
Ellen dithered around her apartment, uncertain how to tackle the family crisis.

■ DIVERGENT—different from another, departing from convention
He held divergent views from the rest of the crowd.

■ DOLT—idiot, dimwit, foolish person
"You dolt," she yelled, spitting out her coffee, "you put salt in the sugar bowl!"

■ DONOR—benefactor, contributor
Blood donors should be tested for diseases before their blood is used in transfusions.

■ DUPE (v.)—to deceive, trick
Bugs Bunny was able to dupe Elmer Fudd by dressing up as a lady rabbit.

■ DUPE (n.)—fool, pawn
But one day, Elmer Fudd decided that he would be Bugs Bunny's dupe no longer; he ripped the lady rabbit's clothes off, only to discover that she was in fact a lady rabbit after all.

■ DUPLICITY—deception, dishonesty, double-dealing
Diplomatic relations between the two superpowers were outwardly friendly, yet characterized by duplicity.

E

■ EBB—to fade away, recede
Melissa enjoyed watching the ebb and flow of the tide from her beachside balcony.

■ EBULLIENT—exhilarated, full of enthusiasm and high spirits
The ebullient child exhausted the babysitter, who lacked the energy to keep up with her.

■ ECLECTIC—selecting from various sources
Budapest's architecture is an eclectic mix of eastern and western styles.

■ EDIFY—to instruct morally and spiritually
The guru was paid to edify the actress in the ways of Buddhism.

■ EFFICACIOUS—effective, efficient
Penicillin was one of the most efficacious drugs on the market when it was first introduced; the drug completely eliminated almost all bacterial infections for which it was administered.

■ EFFIGY—stuffed doll; likeness of a person
The anti-American militants burned Uncle Sam in effigy during their demonstration.

■ EFFULGENT—brilliantly shining
The effulgent angel hovering in the dark evening sky dazzled the sharecroppers.

■ EFFUSIVE—expressing emotion without restraint
The teacher praised Brian effusively for his brilliant essay.

■ EGREGIOUS—conspicuously bad
The English text book contained several egregious errors; for example, "grammar" was misspelled as "gramer" throughout.

■ ELEGY—mournful poem, usually about the dead
Although Thomas Gray's "Elegy Written in a Country Churchyard" is about death and loss, it urges readers to endure life and to trust in spirituality.

■ EMINENT—celebrated, distinguished; outstanding, towering
They were amazed that such an eminent scholar could have made such an obvious error.

■ EMOLLIENT—having soothing qualities, especially for skin
After using the emollient lotion for a couple of weeks, Donna's skin changed from scaly to smooth.

■ EMPATHY—identification with another's feelings
Having taught English herself, Julie felt a strong empathy for the troubled English teacher in the film.

■ EMULATE—to copy, imitate
The graduate student sought to emulate the professor he admired.

■ ENCORE—additional performance, often demanded by audience
The soprano performed three encores, much to the delight of the enthusiastic audience.

■ ENDEMIC—belonging to a particular area, inherent
Bats are usually endemic to caves, so I was surprised to see one flying above the field.

- **ENERVATE**—to weaken, sap strength from
The guerrillas hoped that a series of surprise attacks would enervate the regular army.

- **ENGENDER**—to produce, cause, bring about
His fear of clowns was engendered when he witnessed the death of his father at the hands of a clown.

- **ENIGMATIC**—puzzling, inexplicable
Because he spoke in riddles and dressed in robes, his peers considered the artist's behavior enigmatic.

- **ENNUI**—boredom, lack of interest and energy
Joe tried to alleviate the ennui he felt while doing his tedious job by joking with his coworkers.

- **ENSCONCE**—to settle comfortably into a place
Wayne sold the big, old family house and ensconced his aged mother in a cozy little cottage.

- **EPHEMERAL**—momentary, transient, fleeting
The lives of mayflies seem ephemeral to us, since the flies' average life span is a matter of hours.

- **EQUINE**—relating to horses
Many donkeys have equine characteristics, although they are not horses.

- **EQUIVOCAL**—ambiguous, open to two interpretations and intended to mislead
When I questioned him about the incident, he gave me an equivocal answer.

- **EQUIVOCATE**—to use vague or ambiguous language intentionally
When faced with criticism of his policies, the politician equivocated and left all parties thinking he agreed with them.

- **ERADICATE**—to erase or wipe out
It is unlikely that poverty will ever be completely eradicated in this country, though the standard of living has significantly improved in recent decades.

- **ERUDITE**—learned, scholarly
The annual meeting of professors brought together the most erudite, respected individuals in the field.

- **ESCHEW**—to abstain from, avoid
Models generally eschew rich desserts because such desserts are fattening.

- **ESOTERIC**—understood by only a learned few
Only a handful of experts are knowledgeable about the esoteric world of particle physics.

- **ETHEREAL**—not earthly, spiritual, delicate
Her delicate, ethereal beauty made her a popular model for Pre-Raphaelite artists.

- **ETHOS**—beliefs or character of a group
In accordance with the ethos of his people, the teenage boy underwent a series of initiation rituals to become a man.

- **EUPHEMISM**—use of an inoffensive word or phrase in place of a more distasteful one
The funeral director preferred to use the euphemism "passed away" instead of the word "dead."

- **EXACERBATE**—to aggravate, intensify the bad qualities of
It is unwise to take aspirin to relieve heartburn; instead of providing relief, the drug will only exacerbate the problem.

- **EXASPERATION**—irritation
The catcher couldn't hide his exasperation when the pitcher refused to listen to his advice, throwing a series of pitches that resulted in home runs for the opposing team.

- **EXCULPATE**—to clear of blame or fault, vindicate
The adversarial legal system is intended to convict those who are guilty and to exculpate those who are innocent.

- **EXEMPLARY**—outstanding, an example to others
His exemplary behavior set a fine example for the rest of the class.

- **EXIGENT**—urgent; excessively demanding
The patient was losing blood so rapidly that it was exigent to stop the source of the bleeding.

- **EXPLODE**—to debunk, disprove; blow up, burst
The "free love" common in the 60's exploded conventional theories of marriage and courtship.

- **EXPOUND**—to elaborate; to expand or increase
The teacher expounded on the theory of relativity for hours, boring his students.

- **EXTOL**—to praise
The salesman extolled the virtues of the used car he was trying to convince the customer to buy.

- **EXTRICATE**—to free from, disentangle
The fly was unable to extricate itself from the flypaper.

F

- **FABRICATE**—to make or devise; construct
  A prefab house is one that is fabricated before it is transported to a plot of land.

- **FACILITY**—aptitude, ease in doing something
  Bob had a facility for trigonometry problems, although he could not do algebra at all.

- **FALLACIOUS**—wrong, unsound, illogical
  We now know that the statement "the earth is flat" is fallacious.

- **FALLOW**—uncultivated, unused
  This field should lie fallow for a year so that the soil does not become completely depleted.

- **FASTIDIOUS**—careful with details
  Brett was normally so fastidious that Rachel was astonished to find his desk littered with clutter.

- **FATUOUS**—stupid; foolishly self-satisfied
  Ted's fatuous comments always embarrassed his keen-witted wife at parties.

- **FAZE**—to bother, upset, or disconcert
  Strangely, the news that his car had been stolen did not faze Nathan, though his wife was hysterical.

- **FECKLESS**—ineffective, careless, irresponsible
  Anja took on the responsibility of caring for her aged mother, realizing that her feckless sister was not up to the task.

- **FECUND**—fertile, fruitful, productive
  The fecund housewife gave birth to a total of twenty children.

- **FEIGN**—to pretend, give a false impression; to invent falsely
  Although Sean feigned indifference, he was very much interested in the contents of the envelope.

- **FELL** (v.)—to chop, cut down
  The muscular logger felled the tree in one powerful blow.

- **FERVID**—passionate, intense, zealous
  The fans of Maria Callas were particularly fervid, doing anything to catch a glimpse of the great singer.

- **FIASCO**—disaster, utter failure
  After the soloist turned up drunk, it was hardly surprising that the concert was an utter fiasco.

- **FINICKY**—fussy, difficult to please
  The finicky child rejected every dish on the menu, to the exasperation of his parents.

- **FLACCID**—limp, flabby, weak
  The woman jiggled her flaccid arms in disgust, resolving to begin lifting weights as soon as possible.

- **FLAUNT**—to show off
  Rhonda flaunted her engagement ring all over the office.

- **FLEDGLING**—young bird just learning to fly; beginner, novice
  The fledgling eagle clung to the edge of the cliff, afraid to take its first plunge into the open air.

- **FORTUITOUS**—happening by luck, fortunate
  Rochelle got her start in the music industry when a powerful agent happened, fortuitously, to attend one of her gigs.

- **FRACAS**—noisy dispute
  As we were just down the hall, we couldn't help but hear the fracas.

- **FRACTIOUS**—unruly, rebellious
  The general had a hard time maintaining discipline among his fractious troops.

- **FRAUGHT**—full of, accompanied by
  The sea voyage was fraught with peril; the crew had to contend with storms, sharks, and scurvy on board.

- **FULSOME**—sickeningly excessive; repulsive
  Diana felt nauseous at the sight of the rich, fulsome dishes weighing down the table at the banquet.

- **FURTIVE**—secret, stealthy
  Glenn furtively peered out of the corner of his eye at the stunningly beautiful model.

G

- **GALL** (n.)—bitterness; careless nerve
  I cannot believe she had the gall to show up late her first day of work.

- **GALL** (v.)—to exasperate and irritate
  My uncle constantly galls my aunt by putting his feet up on the coffee table.

- GARRULOUS—very talkative
The garrulous parakeet distracted its owner with its continuous talking.

- GNOSTIC—having to do with knowledge
The Gnostics were distrusted by the Church because of their preference for knowledge over faith.

- GRANDIOSE—magnificent and imposing; exaggerated and pretentious
The house had a grandiose facade that disguised its humble and simple interior.

- GRASP (v.)—to perceive and understand; to hold securely
Peggy could not grasp the concept that Dwight had dumped her, and she continued to call him every day.

- GREGARIOUS—outgoing, sociable
She was so gregarious that when she found herself alone she felt quite sad.

- GRIMACE—facial expression showing pain or disgust
The count grimaced when his wife, drunk as usual, spilled a carafe of wine on the King.

- GROSS (n.)—total before deductions
The company's gross earnings exceeded its predictions.

- GUILE—trickery, deception
Greg used considerable guile to acquire his rent-controlled apartment.

H

- HABITAT—dwelling place
A rabbit's habitat should be a large, dry area with plenty of food, water, and hay available.

- HACKNEYED—worn out by overuse
We always mock my father for his hackneyed expressions and dated hairstyle.

- HAPLESS—unfortunate, having bad luck
I wish someone would give that poor, hapless soul some food and shelter.

- HASTEN—to hurry, to speed up
Juanita hastened to the post office to send off her presents in time for Christmas.

- HEDONISM—pursuit of pleasure as a goal
Michelle lay on the couch eating cookies all day, claiming hedonism was her philosophy of life.

- HEGEMONY—leadership, domination, usually by a country
When Germany claimed hegemony over Russia, Stalin was outraged.

- HEINOUS—shocking, wicked, terrible
Nobody could believe the heinous act the criminal had committed.

- HOMAGE—public honor and respect
Upon arriving at the village, the warriors paid homage to its chief.

- HONE—to sharpen
You might want to hone your writing skills before filling out college applications.

- HUSBAND (v.)—to farm; manage carefully and thriftily
The farmer's wife husbanded the money she had made from her strawberry preserves throughout the year.

- HYPERBOLE—purposeful exaggeration for effect
When the mayor claimed his town was one of the seven wonders of the world, outsiders classified his statement as hyperbole.

I

- ICONOCLAST—one who attacks traditional beliefs
His lack of regard for traditional beliefs soon established him as an iconoclast.

- IGNOMINIOUS—disgraceful and dishonorable
He was humiliated by his ignominious dismissal.

- ILK—type or kind
"I try not to associate with men of his ilk," sniffed the respectable old lady.

- ILLUSTRIOUS—famous, renowned
The illustrious composer produced masterpiece after masterpiece, entrancing her fans.

- IMBUE—to infuse; dye, wet, moisten
Marcia struggled to imbue her children with decent values, a difficult task in this day and age.

- IMMUTABLE—unchangeable, invariable
Public disclosure of personal information now seems to be an immutable fact of campaigning.

■ IMPEACH—to charge with misdeeds in public office; accuse
The senators debated whether or not the president should be impeached for his crimes.

■ IMPECUNIOUS—poor, having no money
After the stock market crashed, many former millionaires found themselves impecunious.

■ IMPERIOUS—arrogantly self-assured, domineering, overbearing
The imperious princess demanded that her servants do back flips every time they came into her presence.

■ IMPERTINENT—rude
The impertinent boy stuck his tongue out at the policeman.

■ IMPERVIOUS—impossible to penetrate; incapable of being affected
A good raincoat should be impervious to moisture.

■ IMPETUOUS—quick to act without thinking
The impetuous day trader rushed to sell his stocks at the first hint of trouble, and lost $300,000.

■ IMPLICIT—implied, not directly expressed
Implicit in Jake's request that Shiela return his keys was his desire to terminate their relationship.

■ IMPORTUNE—to ask repeatedly, beg
The assistant importuned her boss with requests for a raise.

■ IMPUGN—to call into question, attack verbally
"How dare you impugn my honorable motives?" protested the lawyer on being accused of ambulance chasing.

■ IMPULSIVE—spontaneous, unpredictable
She was on her way to London, but at the last minute she impulsively canceled the trip and went to Hawaii instead.

■ INANE—foolish, silly, lacking significance
The talk show host desperately tried to make the star's inane comments seem more interesting.

■ INCANDESCENT—shining brightly
The moon had an incandescent glow on that romantic night we met.

■ INCARCERATE—to put in jail; to confine
The thief was incarcerated for two years, but he got out on parole after six months.

■ INCENSE (v.)—to infuriate, enrage
The general became thoroughly incensed when his subordinates failed to follow his orders.

■ INCHOATE—imperfectly formed or formulated
As her thoughts on the subject were still inchoate, Amy could not explain what she meant.

■ INCISIVE—perceptive, penetrating
The psychologist's incisive analysis of her patient's childhood helped him to understand his own behavior.

■ INCLINATION—tendency towards
Her natural inclination was to refuse Max's invitation to dinner, but since he was her boss she felt obligated to accept it.

■ INCORRIGIBLE—incapable of being corrected
The puppy was incorrigible; however many times he was told not to chew on his master's shoes, he persisted in doing it.

■ INCULPATE—to blame, charge with a crime
His suspicious behavior after the crime tended to inculpate him.

■ INDIGENT—very poor
Because the suspect was indigent, the state paid for his legal representation.

■ INDIGNANT—angry, incensed, offended
The innocent passerby was indignant when the police treated him as a suspect in the crime.

■ INDOLENT—habitually lazy, idle
Her indolent ways got her fired from many jobs.

■ INDUBITABLE—unquestionable
His indubitable cooking skills made it all the more astonishing when the Thanksgiving dinner he prepared tasted awful.

■ INEBRIATED—drunk, intoxicated
Obviously inebriated, the best man slurred his words during his speech at the wedding.

■ INEVITABLE—certain, unavoidable
With many obstacles to deal overcome, it seemed inevitable that their relationship would end.

■ INEXORABLE—inflexible, unyielding
The inexorable force of the twister swept away their house.

■ INFALLIBLE—incapable of making a mistake
I considered my mother to be infallible until she burned the entire dinner.

■ INFER—to conclude, deduce
I think we can infer from the results of this survey that the quality of old age homes needs to be improved.

■ INFAMOUS—famous for having committed bad deeds
He was infamous for all of the crimes he had committed.

■ INGENUOUS—straightforward, open; naive and unsophisticated
She was so ingenuous that her friends feared her innocence would be exploited when she visited the big city.

■ INGRATIATE—to bring oneself purposely into another's good graces
Walter ingratiated himself with his new coworkers by bringing them doughnuts every morning.

■ INIMICAL—hostile, unfriendly
Even though a cease-fire had been in place for months, the two sides were still inimical to each other.

■ INNOCUOUS—harmless; inoffensive
Some snakes are poisonous, but most are innocuous and pose no danger to humans.

■ INNOVATE—to invent, modernize, revolutionize
Coco Chanel innovated a popular new suit design, transforming the fashion industry.

■ INSIDIOUS—sly, treacherous, devious
Iago's insidious comments about Desdemona fueled Othello's feelings of jealousy regarding his wife.

■ INSIPID—bland, lacking flavor; lacking excitement
The critic claimed that the soup was insipid, lacking any type of flavor.

■ INSOLENT—insulting and arrogant
"How dare you, insolent wretch!" roared the King when the peasant laughed at the sight of him stumbling into the mud.

■ INSULAR—isolated, detached
The inhabitants of the insular little village were shocked when Mrs. Malone set up a belly-dancing school in her home.

■ INTRANSIGENT—uncompromising, refusing to be reconciled
The professor was intransigent on the deadline, insisting that everyone turn the assignment in on Friday.

■ INTREPID—fearless
The intrepid hiker completed his ascent to the peak, despite the freezing winds that cut through his body.

■ INURE—to harden; accustom; become used to
Eventually, Hassad became inured to the sirens that went off every night.

■ INVALIDATE—to negate or nullify
Niko's driver's license was invalidated after he was caught speeding in a school zone.

■ INVECTIVE—verbal abuse
A stream of invective poured from Mrs. Pratt's mouth as she watched the vandals smash her ceramic frog.

■ INVIDIOUS—envious; tending to rouse ill will or resentment
Her actions were cruel and invidious.

■ INVINCIBLE—invulnerable, unbeatable
At the height of his career, Mike Tyson was considered practically invincible.

■ IOTA—very tiny amount
"If I even got one iota of respect from you, I'd be satisfied!" raged the father at his insolent son.

■ IRASCIBLE—easily angered
Attila the Hun's irascible and violent nature made all who dealt with him fear for their lives.

■ IRRESOLVABLE—unable to be resolved; not analyzable
The conflict between Catholics and Protestants in Northern Ireland seemed irresolvable until just recently.

■ IRREVERENT—disrespectful, gently or humorously mocking
Kevin's irreverent attitude in Sunday School annoyed the priest, but amused the other children.

■ ITINERANT—wandering from place to place, unsettled
The itinerant salesman came by the Johansson homestead every six months or so.

J

- JADED—tired by excess or overuse; slightly cynical
  While the naive girls stared at the spectacle in awe, the jaded matrons dozed in their chairs.
- JOCULAR—jovial, playful, humorous
  The jocular old man entertained his grandchildren with jokes for hours.
- JUBILEE—special anniversary
  At the Queen's Silver Jubilee, the entire country celebrated her long reign.
- JUDICIOUS—sensible, showing good judgment
  The wise and distinguished judge was well known for having a judicious temperament.
- JUGGERNAUT—huge force destroying everything in its path
  The juggernaut of Napoleon's army surged ahead until it was halted in its tracks by the brutal winter.

K

- KEEN—having a sharp edge; intellectually sharp, perceptive
  With her keen intelligence, she figured out the puzzle in seconds flat.
- KINDLE—to set fire to or ignite; excite or inspire
  With only damp wood to work with, Tilda had trouble kindling the camp fire.
- KUDOS—fame, glory, honor
  The actress happily accepted kudos from the press for her stunning performance.

L

- LACHRYMOSE—tearful
  Heather always became lachrymose when it was time to bid her daughter goodbye.
- LACKADAISICAL—idle, lazy; apathetic, indifferent
  The clerk yawned openly in the customer's face, not bothering to hide his lackadaisical attitude.
- LACONIC—using few words
  She was a laconic poet who built her reputation on using words sparingly.

- LAMPOON—to attack with satire, mock harshly
  The mayor hated being lampooned by the press for his efforts to make the inhabitants of his city more polite.
- LANGUID—lacking energy, indifferent, slow
  The cat languidly cleaned its fur, ignoring the viciously snarling dog chained nearby.
- LASSITUDE—lethargy, sluggishness
  The defeated French army plunged into a state of depressed lassitude as they trudged home from Russia.
- LATENT—present but hidden; potential
  Milton's latent paranoia began to emerge as he was put under more and more stress at the office.
- LAUDABLE—deserving of praise
  Kristin's dedication is laudable, but she doesn't have the necessary skills to be a good paralegal.
- LEGERDEMAIN—trickery
  The magician was skilled in the arts of legerdemain.
- LETHARGY—indifferent inactivity
  The worker sank into a state of lethargy, letting dozens of defective toys pass him by on the assembly line.
- LEXICON—dictionary, list of words
  You may not find the word "supercalifragilisticexpialidocious" in the lexicon.
- LIBERAL—tolerant, broad-minded; generous, lavish
  Kate's liberal parents trusted her, and allowed her to manage her own affairs to a large extent.
- LICENTIOUS—immoral; unrestrained by society
  Religious citizens were outraged by the licentious exploits of the artists living among them.
- LIONIZE—to treat as a celebrity
  After the success of his novel, the author was lionized by the press.
- LISSOME—easily flexed, limber, agile
  The lissome yoga instructor twisted herself into shapes that her students could only dream of.
- LISTLESS—lacking energy and enthusiasm
  Listless and depressed after breaking up with his girlfriend, Nick spent his days moping on the couch.
- LOATHE—to abhor, despise, hate
  Stuart loathed the subject so much that he could barely stand to sit through his physics class.

■ LONGEVITY—long life
With the help of good genes, longevity ran in his family.

■ LOQUACIOUS—talkative
She was naturally loquacious, which was a problem in situations where she was required to listen.

■ LUGUBRIOUS—sorrowful, mournful; dismal
The old woman's lugubrious face depressed everyone who spent time with her.

■ LURID—harshly shocking, sensational; glowing
The politician nearly had a heart attack when he saw the lurid headlines about his past indiscretions.

M

■ MAELSTROM—whirlpool; turmoil; agitated state of mind
The transportation system of the city had collapsed in the maelstrom of war.

■ MAGNANIMOUS—generous, noble in spirit
Although at first he seemed unkind, Uncle Frank turned out to be a very magnanimous fellow.

■ MALADROIT—clumsy, tactless
"Gee, the chili tastes funny," said the maladroit guest to his hostess.

■ MALADY—illness
Elizabeth visited the doctor many times, but he could not identify her mysterious malady.

■ MALAPROPISM—humorous misuse of a word
When the toddler pointed to the puppy and said, "Look at the fluffy," his malapropism delighted his parents.

■ MALCONTENT—discontented person, one who holds a grudge
Dinah had always been a malcontent, so no one was surprised when she complained about the new carpet in the lobby.

■ MALEDICTION—curse
The prince/frog looked for a princess to kiss him and put an end to the witch's evil malediction.

■ MALEVOLENT—ill-willed; causing evil or harm to others
The malevolent woman unfairly spread false rumors about her teammate.

■ MALINGER—to evade responsibility by pretending to be ill
Malingering is a common way to avoid the military draft.

■ MALODOROUS—foul smelling
The malodorous beggar, who had not bathed in many months, could barely stand his own smell.

■ MANIFEST (adj.)—obvious
The fact that she had had plastic surgery was manifest, since she looked 20 years younger than she had the week before.

■ MANUAL (adj.)—hand operated; physical
When the power lines went down, the writer dug out his old manual typewriter to type his script.

■ MARTINET—strict disciplinarian, one who rigidly follows rules
A complete martinet, the administrator insisted that Pete fill out all the forms again even though he was already familiar with his case.

■ MAUDLIN—overly sentimental
The mother's death should have been a touching scene, but the movie's treatment of it was so maudlin that, instead of making the audience cry, it made them cringe.

■ MAWKISH—sickeningly sentimental
The poet hoped to charm his lover with his romantic poem, but its mawkish tone sickened her instead.

■ MEGALOMANIA—mental state in which delusions of wealth and power predominate
Suffering from megalomania, the man constantly talked about how he alone had been responsible for the success of the project.

■ MELANCHOLY—sadness, depression
The gloomy, rainy weather made James feel melancholy.

■ MENDACIOUS—dishonest
So many of her stories were mendacious that I decided she must be a pathological liar.

■ MENDICANT—beggar
"Please, sir, can you spare a dime?" begged the mendicant as the businessman walked past.

■ MERCURIAL—quick, shrewd, and unpredictable
Her mercurial personality made it difficult to guess how she would react to the bad news.

■ MERITORIOUS—deserving reward or praise
The student's performance in all subjects was so meritorious that I'm sure she'll be awarded a scholarship.

■ MIRTH—frivolity, gaiety, laughter
Vera's hilarious jokes contributed to the general mirth at the dinner party.

■ MISANTHROPE—person who hates human beings
Scrooge was such a misanthrope that even the sight of children singing made him angry.

■ MITIGATE—to soften, or make milder
A judge may mitigate a sentence if he or she decides that a crime was committed out of need.

■ MOCK—to deride, ridicule
Charles suspected that Toni was mocking him behind his back, but in fact, she respected him greatly.

■ MOLLIFY—to calm or make less severe
Their disagreement was so intense that it was difficult to believe a compromise would mollify them.

■ MORIBUND—dying, decaying
Thanks to the feminist movement, many sexist customs are now moribund in this society.

■ MOROSE—gloomy, sullen, or surly
After hearing that he had been rejected by the university of his choice, Lenny was morose for weeks.

■ MORSEL—small bit of food
The timid bird darted forward and grabbed the morsel of food from the girl's fingers.

■ MULTIFARIOUS—diverse
Ken opened the hotel room window, letting in the multifarious noises of the great city.

■ MUNIFICENT—generous
The munificent millionaire donated ten million dollars to the hospital.

■ MYOPIC—nearsighted; narrow-minded
The myopic old man needed a magnifying glass to read the morning paper.

N

■ NADIR—lowest point
As Lou waited in line to audition for the diaper commercial, he realized he had reached the nadir of his acting career.

■ NASCENT—starting to develop, coming into existence
The advertising campaign was still in a nascent stage, and nothing had been finalized.

■ NEFARIOUS—vicious, evil
Nefarious deeds are never far from an evil-doer's mind.

■ NEONATE—newborn child
The intensive care unit was filled with tiny, vulnerable neonates having respiratory problems.

■ NOISOME—stinking, putrid
A dead mouse trapped in your walls produces a noisome odor.

■ NOVITIATE—state of being a beginner or novice
Women who want to enter a convent must go through a lengthy novitiate before they can be accepted as full-fledged nuns.

■ NOXIOUS—harmful, unwholesome
The workers wore face masks to avoid breathing in the noxious chemical fumes.

■ NUTRITIVE—relating to nutrition or health
Try as he might, George could not tempt us to eat the seaweed, despite its nutritive value.

O

■ OBDURATE—stubborn
The President was obdurate on the issue, and no amount of persuasion would change his mind.

■ OBFUSCATE—to confuse, obscure
Benny always obfuscates his own arguments by using complicated words that he doesn't understand.

■ OBSEQUIOUS—overly submissive, brownnosing, fawning
The obsequious new employee complimented her supervisor's tie and agreed with him on every issue.

- OBSEQUY—funeral ceremony
The obsequy was solemn.

- OBSTREPEROUS—troublesome, boisterous, unruly
The obstreperous toddler, who was always breaking things, was the terror of his nursery school.

- OBTRUSIVE—pushy, too conspicuous
I think that huge portrait of yourself that you hung in the hall is a bit obtrusive, don't you?

- OBVIATE—to make unnecessary; to anticipate and prevent
The river was shallow enough for the riders to wade across, which obviated the need for a bridge.

- ODIOUS—hateful, contemptible
While most people consider studying vocabulary an odious task, there are a few who find it enjoyable.

- OFFICIOUS—too helpful, meddlesome
The officious waiter interrupted the couple's conversation to advise them on how to take out a mortgage.

- OMNIPOTENT—having unlimited power
The manager clearly thinks he is omnipotent in the way he orders everyone around.

- OPINE—to express an opinion
The audience member of the talk show opined that the guest was a pathetic excuse for a human being.

- OPPORTUNIST—one who takes advantage of circumstances
Dozens of opportunists traveled to the earthquake-stricken region to sell food and water to the victims.

- OPULENCE—wealth
Livingston considered his sports car to be a symbol of both opulence and style.

- ORATION—lecture, formal speech
The class valedictorian gave an impressive oration on graduation day.

- ORATOR—lecturer, speaker
The professor's dull tone of voice and lack of energy make her a particularly poor orator.

- ORDAIN—to make someone a priest or minister; to order
Stephanie proudly watched as her mother was ordained the first female minister in the church's history.

- OSCILLATE—to move back and forth
The fans, oscillating from the ceiling, did little to cool down the humid Florida restaurant.

- OSTENTATIOUS—showy
The billionaire's 200-room palace was considered by many to be an overly ostentatious display of wealth.

P

- PALATIAL—like a palace, magnificent
Carla had lived in a studio apartment for five lean years, and so her new one-bedroom seemed downright palatial by comparison.

- PALLID—lacking color or liveliness
After spending the entire winter indoors, he seemed more pallid than usual.

- PALPABLE—obvious, real, tangible
As soon as Nicola disembarked from the plane in Mexico City, she noticed a palpable difference in the humidity.

- PANEGYRIC—elaborate praise; formal hymn of praise
In praise of the man who had donated a lot of money to the charity, the director launched into a panegyric.

- PARADIGM—ideal example, model
The small restaurant owner used McDonalds as a paradigm for the expansion of his business.

- PARIAH—outcast
After it was discovered that he had misled them for his own profit, he was labelled a pariah in the community.

- PAROCHIAL—limited in scope or outlook, provincial
It was obvious that Victor's parochial mentality would clash with Ivonne's liberal open-mindedness.

- PARSIMONY—stinginess
Although the old woman was considered wealthy by any standard, she still had a reputation for parsimony.

- PASTICHE—piece of literature or music imitating or made up of other works
The playwright's clever pastiche of the well-known Bible story had the audience rolling in the aisles.

- PAUCITY—scarcity, lack
  The paucity of bananas in the country caused their price to skyrocket.

- PECCADILLO—minor sin or offense
  Gabriel unfairly harps on his brother's peccadilloes.

- PEDESTRIAN (adj.)—commonplace
  Although the restaurant had high prices, critics considered its food little more than pedestrian.

- PEJORATIVE—having bad connotations; disparaging
  The teacher scolded Mark for making pejorative comments about his classmate's presentation.

- PELLUCID—transparent; translucent; easily understood
  We couldn't determine whether the pellucid liquid in the bottle was water or vodka.

- PENCHANT—inclination
  Tiffany's penchant for fine dining made her thrifty husband a bit uncomfortable.

- PENULTIMATE—next to last
  The penultimate syllable in the word "pellucid" is stressed.

- PERDITION—complete and utter loss; damnation
  Faust brought perdition upon himself when he made a deal with the Devil in exchange for power.

- PERFIDIOUS—faithless, disloyal, untrustworthy
  The actress's perfidious companion revealed all of her intimate secrets to the gossip columnist.

- PERFUNCTORY—done in a routine way; indifferent
  The machinelike bank teller processed the transaction and gave the customer a perfunctory smile.

- PERIPATETIC—moving from place to place
  Morty enjoys his peripatetic life; every day, he moves his hot dog stand to a different part of the city.

- PERNICIOUS—very harmful
  The Claytons considered acid rock music to be a pernicious influence on their impressionable daughter.

- PERSPICACIOUS—shrewd, astute, keen witted
  Inspector Poirot used his perspicacious mind to solve mysteries.

- PERUSAL—close examination
  When you fly, your carry-on luggage is subject to the perusal of customs officials.

- PHILANDERER—pursuer of casual love affairs
  The philanderer, incapable of being faithful to just one woman, had been through several divorces.

- PHLEGMATIC—calm in temperament; sluggish
  The phlegmatic old boar snoozed in the grass as the energetic piglets frolicked around him.

- PINNACLE—peak, highest point of development
  The entire show was excellent, but the pinnacle was when the skater did a backward flip.

- PIOUS—dedicated, devout, extremely religious
  Saul, a pious man, walks to the synagogue on the Sabbath and prays daily.

- PITHY—profound, substantial; concise, succinct, to the point
  Martha's pithy comments during the interview must have been impressive, because she got the job.

- PLATITUDE—stale, overused expression
  Although Jacob has some interesting ideas, he relies too much on platitudes in his writing.

- PLIANT—pliable, yielding
  Only those with extremely pliant limbs are able to perform complex yoga moves.

- PLUCKY—courageous, spunky
  The plucky young nurse dove bravely into the foxhole, determined to save the soldier's life.

- PLUMMET—to fall, plunge
  She watched in horror as her ring plummeted down the cliff.

- PONDEROUS—weighty, heavy, large
  We reflected on the ponderous issue, "What is the meaning of life?"

- PORTENTOUS—ominous
  Kylie quaked in fear as she watched a black cat cross her path, a portentous sign.

- PORTLY—stout, dignified
  The portly man wearily put on the Santa suit and set out for the mall.

- PRAGMATIC—practical; moved by facts rather than abstract ideals
  Growing up, I was considered the daydreamer while my sister was the pragmatic one.

- PRECARIOUS—uncertain
The mountain goat almost lost its precarious footing on the cliff face.

- PRECLUDE—to rule out
The seriousness of the car's damage precluded any possibility of repairing it.

- PRECOCIOUS—unusually advanced at an early age
The fact that Beatrice got married at age eighteen did not come as much of a shock, as she had always been precocious.

- PREDICAMENT—difficult situation
Because he had spent all of his pay, Sean found himself in a miserable predicament when his rent bill arrived.

- PREDILECTION—preference, liking
Susie's predilection for candy was evident from the chocolate bar wrappers strewn all over her apartment.

- PRESCIENT—having foresight
Jonah's decision to sell the apartment turned out to be a prescient one, as its value soon dropped by half.

- PRESUMPTUOUS—rude, improperly bold
"I don't want to be presumptuous, but why on earth did you choose red wallpaper?" said Ceci to her hosts.

- PRETENTIOUS—pretending to be important, intelligent or cultured
Pretentious people pretend to be important.

- PREVARICATE—to lie, evade the truth
Rather than admit he had overslept again, the employee prevaricated, claiming that traffic had made him late.

- PRIMEVAL—ancient, primitive
The archaeologist claimed that the skeleton was of primeval origin, though in actuality it was the remains of a monkey who had recently died at the zoo.

- PRIVATION—lack of usual necessities or comforts
The convict endured total privation while locked up in solitary confinement for a month.

- PROCLIVITY—tendency, inclination
His proclivity for speeding got him into trouble with the highway patrol on many occasions.

- PROCRASTINATOR—one who continually and unjustifiably postpones
Don't be a procrastinator; do your homework now!

- PRODIGIOUS—vast, enormous, extraordinary
The musician's prodigious talent made her famous all over the world.

- PROFICIENT—expert, skilled in a certain subject
The mechanic was proficient at repairing cars, but his horrible temper made it difficult for him to keep jobs for long.

- PROFLIGATE—corrupt, degenerate
Some historians claim that it was the Romans' decadent, profligate behavior that led to the decline of the Roman Empire.

- PROFUSE—lavish, extravagant
Although Janet was angry at Bart for forgetting her birthday, his profuse apologies made her forgive him.

- PROLIFIC—productive, fertile
Stephen King, a prolific writer, seems to come out with a new book every six months.

- PROPINQUITY—nearness
The house's propinquity to the foul-smelling pig farm made it impossible to sell.

- PROPITIATE—to win over, appease
The management propitiated the irate union by agreeing to raise wages for its members.

- PROPONENT—advocate, defender, supporter
A proponent of animal rights, Willy rescued stray cats and dogs whenever he had the chance.

- PROSAIC—relating to prose; dull, commonplace
Simon found the book's prosaic style so uninspiring that he had to force himself to finish reading it.

- PROSCRIBE—to condemn; to forbid, outlaw
Treason was proscribed in the country's constitution.

- PROSECUTOR—person who initiates a legal action or suit
The prosecutor's aggressive questioning left the defendant flustered, which weakened the defense's case.

- PROSPERITY—wealth or success
Cheaters never prosper; honesty and hard work bring prosperity.

- PROTRACT—to prolong, draw out, extend
Since every member of the committee had to have his or her say, the meeting was a protracted affair.

- PROVINCIAL—rustic, unsophisticated, limited in outlook
Anita, a sophisticated city girl, sneered at the provincial attitudes of her country cousins.

- PROWESS—bravery, skill
She credited her athletic prowess to daily practice and intense concentration.

- PRUDENT—wise, sensible
Since our army is so small, it would not be prudent to attack the enemy right now.

- PUERILE—childish, immature, silly
Sam's puerile antics are really annoying; sometimes he acts like a five-year-old!

- PUDGY—chubby, overweight
The pudgy dachshund was quickly put on a diet.

- PUGNACIOUS—quarrelsome, eager and ready to fight
The serene eighty-year-old used to be a pugnacious trouble maker in her youth, but she's softer now.

- PULCHRITUDE—beauty
The mortals gazed in admiration at Venus, stunned by her incredible pulchritude.

- PULVERIZE—to pound, crush, or grind into powder; destroy
The polar bear's awesome strength was such that a single blow from its paw would pulverize a human.

- PUNGENT—strong or sharp in smell or taste
The smoke from the burning tires was extremely pungent.

N

- QUACK—faker; one who falsely claims to have medical skill
The woman had unwittingly gone to a quack for her leg problem.

- QUADRILATERAL—four-sided polygon
The fortress was shaped as a quadrilateral, with watch towers in each of its four corners.

- QUADRUPED—animal having four feet
After I hurt my back, the only way I could move around was to clamber about on all fours like a quadruped.

- QUANDARY—dilemma, difficulty
Bill found himself in a quandary when he realized that he had promised the job to two different applicants.

- QUELL—to crush or subdue
The dictator dispatched troops to quell the rebellion.

- QUERULOUS—inclined to complain, irritable
Curtis's querulous behavior earned him a reputation as the company troublemaker.

- QUIESCENCE—inactivity, stillness
Bears typically fall into a state of quiescence when they hibernate during the winter months.

- QUIVER—to shake slightly, tremble, vibrate
The quivering mobile unfastened from its weak nail and came crashing down.

- QUIXOTIC—overly idealistic, impractical
The practical Danuta was skeptical of her roommate's quixotic plans to build a rollercoaster in their yard.

- QUOTIDIAN—occurring daily; commonplace
The sight of people singing on the street is such a part of quotidian life that New Yorkers rarely react to it anymore.

R

- RACONTEUR—witty, skillful storyteller
The raconteur kept all the passengers entertained with his stories during the six-hour flight.

- RAIL (v.)—to scold with bitter or abusive language
When the teacher assigned twice as much homework as usual, his students railed against such an impossible work load.

- RANCOR—bitter hatred
Herbert was so filled with rancor that he could think of nothing but taking revenge on those who had humiliated him.

- RANT—to harangue, rave, forcefully scold
The teenager barely listened as her father ranted on about her disrespectful behavior.

- **RAPPORT**—relationship of trust and respect
Initially, they disliked one another, but working together eventually forged a rapport between the two men.

- **RAPT**—deeply absorbed
Surprisingly, the normally wild infant sat rapt during the classical music performance.

- **RAREFY**—to make thinner, purer, or more refined
The atmosphere rarefies as altitude increases, so the air at the top of high mountains is too thin to breathe.

- **RASH** (adj.)—careless, hasty, reckless
Lewis rashly jumped to the conclusion that the employee was completely incompetent after she made a small error.

- **RAUCOUS**—harsh sounding; boisterous
The grade school cafeteria was a raucous place at lunch time.

- **RAVENOUS**—extremely hungry
The refugee had not had a bite of food for days and was ravenous.

- **RECALCITRANT**—resisting authority or control
The recalcitrant mule refused to go down the treacherous path, however hard its master pulled at its reins.

- **RECANT**—to retract a statement, opinion, etc.
Even after he tried to recant the words, the statement had been so damning that the politician's credibility was ruined.

- **RECAPITULATE**—to review by a brief summary
After the long-winded president had finished his speech, his assistant recapitulated the points he had made.

- **RECEPTIVE**—open to others' ideas; congenial
The leading software company was receptive to suggestions and new ideas.

- **RECLUSIVE**—shut off from the world
Anthony's reclusive tendencies led him to leave the city and move into a lonely cabin in Montana.

- **RECTIFY**—to correct
Most people would rectify errors they had made if they were given the opportunity.

- **REFORM**—to change, correct
The new mayor struggled to reform the corrupt government, as she had promised the voters she would.

- **REJUVENATE**—to make young again; renew
Martina looked and felt completely rejuvenated after her plastic surgery was completed.

- **RELISH** (v.)—to enjoy greatly
Cameron relished the tasty sandwich, but he didn't like the pickle that came with it.

- **REMUNERATION**—pay or reward for work, trouble, etc.
You can't expect people to do this kind of boring work without some form of remuneration.

- **RENOWN**—fame, widespread acclaim
Having spent her whole childhood banging on things, Jane grew up to be a drummer of great renown.

- **REPLETE**—abundantly supplied
The gigantic supermarket was replete with consumer products of every kind.

- **REPLICATE**—to duplicate, repeat
If we're going to replicate last year's profit margins, we'll have to work very hard.

- **REPUDIATE**—to reject as having no authority
The old woman's claim that she was Russian royalty was repudiated when a DNA match proved negative.

- **RESCIND**—to repeal, cancel
The car company rescinded its promotional offer for a free car.

- **RESILIENT**—able to recover quickly after illness or bad luck; able to bounce back to shape
Luckily, Ramon was resilient, and was able to pick up the pieces after losing his business.

- **RESOLVE** (n.)—determination, firmness of purpose
I admire your resolve, but is it really a good idea to go through with the marathon in this bad weather?

- **RESPLENDENT**—splendid, brilliant
The bride looked resplendent in her long train and sparkling tiara.

- **RESTRAINED**—controlled, repressed, restricted
The girl became more restrained and serious after a month in the strict boarding school.

■ RETICENT—not speaking freely; reserved
Physically small and reticent, the journalist went unnoticed by those upon whom she was reporting.

■ REVELRY—boisterous festivity
An atmosphere of revelry filled the school after its basketball team's surprising victory.

■ REVILE—to criticize with harsh language, verbally abuse
Resentful of the traumas she had inflicted upon him, George reviled his mother at every opportunity.

■ REVITALIZE—to renew; give new energy to
The new CEO's upbeat, supportive managerial style revitalized the previously demoralized staff.

■ REVULSION—strong feeling of repugnance or dislike
Rebecca was filled with revulsion at the stench that the rotten melon in her refrigerator gave off.

■ RIBALD—humorous in a vulgar way
The court jester's ribald brand of humor delighted the rather uncouth King.

■ RUMINATE—to contemplate, reflect upon
The scholars spent days at the retreat, ruminating upon the complexities of the geopolitical situation.

■ RUSTIC—rural
The rustic cabin was an ideal setting for a vacation in the country.

S

■ SACCHARINE—excessively sweet or sentimental
Geoffrey's saccharine love poems nauseated Lucy, and she wished he'd stop sending them.

■ SAGACITY—wisdom, sound judgment
When she faced a problem, she consulted the old man, renowned for his sagacity.

■ SALIENT—prominent or conspicuous
His most salient characteristic is his tendency to dominate every conversation.

■ SALUBRIOUS—healthful
Rundown and sickly, Rita hoped that the fresh mountain air would have a salubrious effect on her health.

■ SANGUINE—ruddy; cheerfully optimistic
A sanguine person thinks the glass is half full, while a pessimistic person sees it as half empty.

■ SARDONIC—cynical, scornfully mocking
Denise was offended by the sardonic way in which her date made fun of her ideas and opinions.

■ SAVORY—agreeable in taste or smell
The banquet guests consumed the savory treats with pleasure.

■ SCINTILLA—trace amount
This poison is so powerful that no more of a scintilla of it is needed to kill a horse.

■ SCORE (n.)—notation for a musical composition
The score of the film was wonderful, but the musicians who performed it were not very skillful.

■ SCORE (v.)—to make a notch or scratch
The prisoner scored a mark in the door for every day he passed in captivity.

■ SCURRILOUS—vulgar, low, indecent
The decadent aristocrat took part in scurrilous activities, unbeknownst to his family.

■ SEDENTARY—inactive, stationary; sluggish
Americans, who often work in sedentary office jobs, are becoming more overweight and out of shape.

■ SEMINAL—relating to the beginning or seeds of something
The professor's theory is regarded as seminal in the discipline, in that many other theories build upon it.

■ SERAPHIC—angelic, pure, sublime
Selena's sweet, seraphic appearance belied her nasty, bitter personality.

■ SERENDIPITY—habit of making fortunate discoveries by chance
It was pure serendipity: while searching for her keys, she found an earring she'd lost a month ago.

■ SERENITY—calm, peacefulness
Lisette's meditation helps her to achieve true serenity.

■ SERVILE—submissive, obedient
As the wealthy widow screamed in rage at him, the servile butler apologized profusely for his mistake.

■ SIMIAN—apelike; relating to apes
Early man was more simian in appearance than modern man, as he was more closely related to apes.

- SLOVENLY—untidy, messy
The cook's clothes were so stained and slovenly that no restaurant would hire him.

- SLUGGARD—lazy, inactive person
Joe considered his friend a sluggard because all he ever seemed to do was watch TV.

- SOBRIQUET—nickname
One of Ronald Reagan's sobriquets was "The Gipper."

- SOMNOLENT—drowsy, sleepy; inducing sleep
Carter became somnolent after taking a couple of sleeping pills.

- SONOROUS—producing a full, rich sound
His sonorous style of speech impressed me greatly.

- SOPHISTRY—deceptive reasoning or argumentation
The politician used sophistry to cloud the issue whenever he was asked a tough question.

- SOPHOMORIC—immature and overconfident
The sophomoric young man was sure he would have no problems in writing the book, although there was no way he could accomplish the task.

- SOPORIFIC—sleepy or tending to cause sleep
The movie proved to be so soporific that soon loud snores were heard throughout the theater.

- SPARTAN—austere, severe, grave; simple, bare
The athlete's room was spartan, containing nothing but a bed and a pair of dumbbells.

- SPONTANEOUS—on the spur of the moment, impulsive
Jean made the spontaneous decision to go to the movies instead of visiting her in-laws as she had planned.

- SPORTIVE—frolicsome, playful
The lion roared in pain as the sportive lion cub bit his tail playfully.

- SPURIOUS—lacking authenticity; counterfeit, false
Reciting a spurious quote, the cult leader declared that all property should be signed over to him.

- SPURN—to reject or refuse contemptuously; scorn
When Harvey proposed to Harriet, she spurned him; she'd always considered him an idiot.

- SQUALID—filthy; morally repulsive
The squalid living conditions in the tenement building outraged the new tenants.

- STALK (v.)—to hunt, pursue
The rock star put a restraining order on the insane woman who had stalked him for many years.

- STOIC—indifferent to or unaffected by emotions
While most of the mourners wept, the dead woman's husband kept up a stoic, unemotional facade.

- STOLID—having or showing little emotion
The defendant appeared stolid and unaffected by the judge's harsh sentence.

- STRIDENT—loud, harsh, unpleasantly noisy
The customer's strident manner annoyed the shop assistant, but she managed to keep her temper.

- STULTIFY—to impair or reduce to uselessness
The company's leadership was stultified by its disregard for organization and efficiency.

- SUBTERRANEAN—hidden, secret; underground
Subterranean passages were dug for the subway after it was decided that there was no longer enough room for the tracks above ground in the crowded city.

- SUCCINCT—terse, brief, concise
She was sought after by many talk shows, as her remarks were always succinct.

- SULLEN—brooding, gloomy
The sullen child sat in the corner by herself, refusing to play with her classmates.

- SUPERSEDE—to take the place of; replace
Word 2000 will gradually supersede older versions of Word on office computers around the world.

- SUPPLICANT—one who asks humbly and earnestly
Alf is normally a cocky fellow, but he transformed himself into a supplicant when he begged the banker for a loan.

- SUPPRESS—to end an activity, e.g., to prevent the dissemination of information
Sue suppressed the urge to press the doorbell for the fifth time.

- SURFEIT—excessive amount
Because of the surfeit of pigs, pork prices have never been lower.

- SURMISE—to make an educated guess
  From his torn pants and bloody nose, I surmised that he had been in a fight.

- SURREPTITIOUS—characterized by secrecy
  The queen knew nothing of the surreptitious plots being hatched against her at court.

- SUSTAIN—support, uphold; endure, undergo
  If we can sustain our efforts a little longer, I'm sure our plan will succeed in the end.

- SYBARITE—person devoted to pleasure and luxury
  A confirmed sybarite, the nobleman fainted at the thought of having to leave the comfort of his palace for that of a small cottage.

- SYCOPHANT—self-serving flatterer, yes-man
  Dreading criticism, the actor surrounded himself with admirers and sycophants.

T

- TACIT—silently understood or implied
  Not a word had been said, but everyone in the room knew that a tacit agreement had been made.

- TACITURN—uncommunicative, not inclined to speak much
  The clerk's taciturn nature earned him the nickname "Silent Sammy."

- TACTFUL—considerate, skillful in acting to avoid offense to others
  A tactful person's actions are in good taste.

- TACTILE—relating to the sense of touch
  She was a very tactile person, constantly touching the objects around her.

- TANGIBLE—able to be sensed, perceptible, measurable
  The storming of the castle didn't bring the soldiers tangible rewards, but it brought them great honor.

- TARNISHED—corroded, discolored; discredited, disgraced
  The antique silver plate was so tarnished that Nestor had to polish it for hours before using it.

- TAWDRY—gaudy, cheap, showy
  The performer changed into her tawdry, spangled costume and stepped out onto the stage to do her show.

- TEMPERANCE—restraint, self-control, moderation
  The strict, religious community frowned on newcomers who did not behave with temperance.

- TEMPESTUOUS—stormy, raging, furious
  Jeannie tried to venture out into the tempestuous storm to buy food, but harsh winds forced her to return home.

- TENACIOUS—stubborn, holding firm
  For years, against all odds, women tenaciously fought for the right to vote.

- TENET—belief, doctrine
  One of the tenets of the Muslim religion is that it is not acceptable to eat pork.

- TENUOUS—weak, insubstantial
  Francine's already tenuous connection to her cousins was broken when they didn't invite her to the party.

- TERRESTRIAL—earthly; down-to-earth, commonplace
  After lengthy investigations, many extraterrestrial objects have proven to be terrestrial in origin.

- TERSE—concise, brief, free of extra words
  Her terse style of writing was widely praised for coming directly to the point.

- TIMOROUS—timid, shy, full of apprehension
  A timorous woman, Lois relied on her children to help her communicate.

- TIRADE—long, violent speech; verbal assault
  Observers were shocked at the manager's tirade over such a minor mistake.

- TOADY—flatterer, hanger-on, yes-man
  The king was surrounded by toadies who rushed to agree with whatever outrageous thing he said.

- TOLERANCE—capacity to respect different values; capacity to endure or resist something
  Dictators are characterized by their lack of tolerance for anyone who opposes them.

- TORPID—lethargic; unable to move; dormant
  After surgery, the patient was torpid until the anesthesia wore off.

- TRACTABLE—obedient, yielding
  Though it was exhausted, the tractable workhorse obediently dragged the carriage through the mud.

- TRANSCEND—to rise above, go beyond
Yoga helps me to transcend the petty frustrations of everyday life and to achieve true spirituality.

- TRANSPIRE—to happen, occur; become known
It later transpired that a faulty gear shift had been responsible for the horrible accident.

- TREPIDATION—fear and anxiety
Mike approached the door of the principal's office with trepidation.

- TRIFLING—of slight worth, trivial, insignificant
That little glitch in the computer program is a trifling error; in general, it works really well.

- TROUPE—group of actors
This acting troupe is famous for its staging of Shakespeare's romantic comedies.

- TRUNCATE—to cut off, shorten by cutting
The mayor truncated his lengthy speech when he realized that the audience was restless.

- TURGID—swollen, bloated
In the process of osmosis, water passes through the walls of turgid cells, ensuring that they never contain too much water.

- TYRO—beginner, novice
An obvious tyro at salsa, Millicent received no invitations to dance.

U

- UBIQUITOUS—being everywhere simultaneously
Burger King franchises are ubiquitous in the United States, and are common in foreign countries as well.

- UMBRAGE—offense, resentment
The businessman took umbrage at the security guard's accusation that he had shoplifted a packet of gum.

- UNANIMITY—state of total agreement or unity
The unanimity of the council on this issue was surprising; I never thought they'd be able to agree on it.

- UNAPPEALING—unattractive, unpleasant
The fish dish looked so unappealing that Laszlo could not bring himself to taste it.

- UNEQUIVOCAL—absolute, certain
The jury's verdict was unequivocal: the sadistic murderer would be locked up for life.

- UNHERALDED—unannounced, unexpected, not publicized
The gallant knight's arrival was unheralded, so the princess was surprised to see him.

- UPBRAID—to scold sharply
The teacher upbraided the student for scrawling graffiti on the walls of the school.

- URBANE—courteous, refined, suave
The urbane teenager sneered at the mannerisms of his country-bumpkin cousin.

- USURP—to seize by force
The vice principal was power hungry, and threatened to usurp the principal's power.

- UTILITARIAN—efficient, functional, useful
The suitcase was undeniably utilitarian, but it was also ugly.

- UTOPIA—perfect place
Wilson's idea of utopia was a beautiful, sunny beach on a tropical island.

V

- VACILLATE—to waver, show indecision
The customer held up the line as he vacillated between ordering chocolate chip or rocky road ice cream.

- VAPID—tasteless, dull
Todd found his blind date vapid, and couldn't wait to get away from her.

- VENERABLE—respected because of age
All of the villagers sought the venerable old woman's advice whenever they had a problem.

- VERACITY—accuracy, truth
She had a reputation for veracity, so everyone believed her version of the story.

- VERBOSE—wordy
The professor's answer was so verbose that his student forgot what the original question had been.

- VERDANT—green with vegetation; inexperienced
He wandered deep into the verdant woods in search of mushrooms and other edible flora.

- VERISIMILITUDE—quality of appearing true or real
  The TV show's verisimilitude led viewers to believe that the characters it portrayed were real.
- VERITY—truthfulness; belief viewed as true and enduring
  The verity of the situation was that Roy couldn't bear to step down and let his sons take over the company.
- VERNAL—related to spring
  Bea basked in the balmy vernal breezes, happy that winter was at last coming to an end.
- VICARIOUS—substitute, surrogate; enjoyed through imagined participation in another's experience
  Harriet lived vicariously through her daughter, listening avidly to her tales of romance and adventure.
- VICISSITUDE—change or variation; ups and downs
  Investors must be prepared for vicissitudes in the stock market.
- VIE—to compete, contend
  The two wrestlers vied for the title of champion in the final match of the competition.
- VIRILE—manly, having qualities of an adult male
  John Wayne tended to play virile, tough roles rather than effeminate, sensitive roles.
- VITRIOLIC—burning, caustic; sharp, bitter
  Given the opportunity to critique his competitor's new book, the spiteful critic wrote an unusually vitriolic review of it for the newspaper.
- VIVID—bright and intense in color; strongly perceived
  The vivid colors of the rose garden were visible from miles away.
- VOLUBLE—speaking much and easily, talkative; glib
  The voluble man and his silent wife proved the old saying that opposites attract.
- VORACIOUS—having a great appetite
  The voracious farming family consumed a huge meal after a long day of heavy labor.

W

- WAN—sickly pale
  The sick child had a wan face, in contrast to her rosy-cheeked sister.
- WANTON—undisciplined, unrestrained, reckless
  Instead of singling out an appropriate target for his anger, the man struck out in a wanton manner.
- WARY—careful, cautious
  The dog was wary of Bola at first, only gradually letting its guard down and wagging its tail when he came home at night.
- WINSOME—charming, happily engaging
  Dawn gave the customs officers a winsome smile, and they let her pass without searching her bags.
- WRY—amusing, ironic
  Although his words sounded very serious, Del's wry expression indicated that he was only joking.

X

- XENOPHOBIA—fear or hatred of foreigners or strangers
  Countries in which xenophobia is prevalent often have more restrictive immigration policies than those that are more accepting of foreign influences.

Y

- YOKE (v.)—to join together
  As soon as the farmer had yoked his oxen together, he began to plow the fields.

Z

- ZEALOT—someone passionately devoted to a cause
  The religious zealot dismissed those who didn't share his beliefs.
- ZENITH—highest point, summit
  The diva considered her performance at the Metropolitan Opera to be the zenith of her career.

KAPLAN

You'll score higher on your SAT IIs.

We guarantee it.

KAPLAN
World Leader In Test Prep

SAT II
U.S. History
2002–2003 EDITION
Higher Score Guaranteed

4 Full-Length Practice Tests
with a detailed explanation for every answer

Comprehensive U.S. History Review
with hundreds of key terms and concepts

Key Strategies to maximize your score

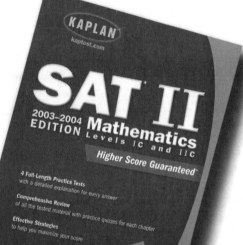

KAPLAN
kaptest.com

SAT II
2003–2004 EDITION
Mathematics Levels IC and IIC

Higher Score Guaranteed

4 Full-Length Practice Tests
with a detailed explanation for every answer

Comprehensive Review
of all the tested material with practice quizzes for each chapter

Effective Strategies
to help you maximize your score

Each guide features:
- **Full-length practice tests**
- **Comprehensive review**
- **Key strategies**

Kaplan also has SAT II guides for:
- **Chemistry**
- **Literature**
- **Physics**
- **Spanish**
- **World History**

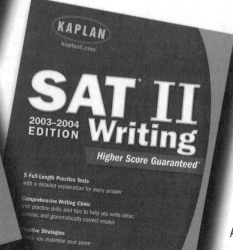

KAPLAN
kaptest.com

SAT II
2003–2004 EDITION
Biology E/M

Higher Score Guaranteed

3 Full-Length Practice Tests
with a detailed explanation for every answer

Comprehensive Review
of all the tested material with practice quizzes for each chapter

Effective Strategies
to help you maximize your score

KAPLAN
kaptest.com

SAT II
2003–2004 EDITION
Writing

Higher Score Guaranteed

5 Full-Length Practice Tests
with a detailed explanation for every answer

Comprehensive Writing Clinic
with practice drills and tips to help you write clear, concise, and grammatically correct essays

Effective Strategies
to help you maximize your score

KAPLAN

Available wherever books are